on the move

Feminism for a New Generation

Edited by Natasha Walter

A *Virago* Book

First published by Virago Press 1999

The collection and introduction copyright ©
Natasha Walter 1999
Copyright © for each contribution is held by the author 1999

The moral rights of the authors have been asserted.

A CIP catalogue record for this book
is available from the British Library

ISBN 186049 321 1

Typeset in Goudy by M Rules
Printed and bound in Great Britain by
Clays Ltd, St Ives plc

Virago Press
A Division of
Little, Brown and Company (UK)
Brettenham House
Lancaster Place
London WC2E 7EN

contents

introduction

Natasha Walter

'I think all women can be feminists.' 'There is still a real agenda for feminism.' 'To me, feminism is about finding equality between men and women in all areas of society.' 'We need feminism now more than ever.' 'Feminism has never been healthier.'

These are some of the statements you'll find in this book. They are statements made by young women – some in their teens, most in their twenties and early thirties. It may come as quite a shock to realise that young women are still so passionate about feminism. When Virago first approached me to edit a book of essays by young women two years ago, I was in the middle of writing my own book, *The New Feminism*. I had just begun to realise that the commitment that many young women felt towards feminism was rarely displayed in the media. It felt to me almost as though there was a hidden desire for feminism, a real pull towards the ideal of a more equal society that was rarely spoken about publicly. And once my book was published, I found that young women in schools and universities and at public meetings reacted to the idea of a refashioned feminism far more positively and with much more excitement than I had ever expected.

I deliberately cast the net wide when choosing the writers for this book, and the women here come from a range of backgrounds. Yet all the writers here feel that feminism is central to their lives. That's telling in itself, because it's not as though these women are alike in any other way. They don't spring from any one background, one class, one political persuasion or one ethnic group, and yet all of them are talking about how feminism can develop in ways that will make sense to a new generation of women.

Many of these writers engage fiercely with the culture and politics that they find around them. Katharine Viner attacks the laddish culture that both encourages women to pose half-naked for men's magazines, and still judges them negatively when they display proactive sexuality. 'Whatever one thinks of Monica Lewinsky,' she notes, 'her story reveals much about the way sexually proactive women are perceived. She was labelled a "sexual initiator" as if the phrase were a slur.' Helen Wilkinson, in her essay on the legacy of Margaret Thatcher, examines the change in attitudes to power among young women. 'We are all,' she observes, 'power feminists now.' Aminatta Forna sets out a blistering attack on the complacency of middle-class women who have declared feminism dead before most women have been able to benefit from its advances, and the novelist Livi Michael takes us into the lives of working-class women to remind us that feminism still has work to do: 'In this class,' she says, 'there are women for whom all the reforms brought about by feminism might as well not exist.'

Some of these women speak about their own personal lives, and how their feminism is spurred on by their individual experiences. Stephanie Theobald writes about how lesbian women still feel invisible. She remembers when she wrote an article called 'How to Make Love to a Woman by a Lesbian' for a leading women's magazine, she found that it curiously mutated into a rather different article called 'Better Sex for Bored Couples'. Jenny McLeod, the playwright and novelist, reaches deep into her mother's life, that of a Jamaican woman who was determined to retain her self-respect even when the men around her seemed to be giving up. 'My mother's two favourite cries are that "no man has ever raised a hand to her" and that "no man has ever come in and asked her where his dinner is,"' she remembers, and she feels that her own feminism was moulded by that fierce independence.

Young women today are living lives that are often quite different from the lives of their mothers or their grandmothers, and the force of change is seen in the work of many of these writers. Helen Simpson explores the dissonance between the optimism of young women and the reality of older women's lives in a memorable short story that gives us Jade Beaumont, a heroine for our times, imagining herself 'moving like a panther into the long jewelled narrative which was her future'. Julie Bindel, a feminist activist who grew up on a working-class estate in north-east England, believes that feminism has transformed her life and the lives of other women on the estate. When she goes back to Darlington, women come up and talk to her on the streets: 'Many say that they have suffered domestic violence, and that hearing or seeing women publicly denouncing violent men has at last given them the strength and confidence they needed to change their lives.' Oona King, the second black woman MP in Britain, tells us what she felt when she was part of the unforgettable surge of women entering Parliament in 1997. 'When I stood on the steps of Church House with 100 other women Labour MPs,' she remembers, 'I knew that our presence in Parliament would mean nothing unless we were able to reduce inequality throughout Britain.'

There is an urgency to many of these essays. We hear again and again from commentators in the media that young women are tired of the struggle for equality, that if anything they feel that feminism has gone too far. But in fact most of these women are eager to see changes, they are eager to move towards a very different society. You can feel their passion and their sense of engagement as they describe both political and personal injustice. These writers are defining a feminism that makes sense to this generation. They may mention Germaine Greer or the Suffragettes or Greenham Common, but they are also eager to explore their own culture. They discuss the relevance of Sara Thornton or Ulrika Jonsson or Mo Mowlam or Bridget Jones, in their efforts to create a feminism that makes sense to themselves and their peers.

When I first read through these essays, I often found myself intrigued and admiring – but I also often disagreed with what the writers chose to say. These are strong views, and no one will agree with everything that everyone says in this book. But despite that there is the possibility of finding common ground and building on it. All the writers here rage against inequality. None of them is complacent. And that lack of complacency, that desire to build a better society in which men and women are more equal, is something that is found all around us now. Although we often hear that young women are tired of feminism, tired of the debate about equality, tired of seeking solutions, the young women in this book show that such counsels of despair may be misplaced. If we listen to one another and enter the debate with open minds, we may find ways of moving on.

As Caroline, the 15-year-old girl whose words close this book says: 'I'm optimistic about the way things are going now. We're coming to a new century and everyone's optimistic about what that will bring. It will be interesting to read this book back in years to come and compare it to what my children's and grandchildren's lives are like. I think I'll look back and see that things have really changed – for the better.'

you go, girl! – young women say there's no holding back

Karen Loughrey (15 years old)

To me, feminism is about finding equality between men and women in all areas of society, from work to family situations, without women being seen as the weaker sex. I personally hold the view that women and men should be equal. I definitely care about feminism, and I think a lot of people still do. I wouldn't call myself an activist, I wouldn't go out protesting and saying burn your bras, because I think that's pathetic. But I think there are a lot of women who are making their position known and making themselves stronger. And feminism is definitely still going on.

The opportunities that I've had are better than my grandmother had at my age. I've had a very good education at a grammar school. My grandmother didn't have that available to her, she left school when she was fourteen. She would have found it hard to get a job, it was a very male-dominated society then. I think she stayed at home with the children, which was the way it was then. But my mum is in a very powerful position – she's a production manager, and she is in control of people, some of which are men. I think she had good opportunities to get where she wanted. Whereas for me, things are even better and whatever I want to do I know that I can go and do it, regardless of whether I'm male or female.

My mum has worked ever since I was young and my nan picked us up from school and that hasn't done anything bad to me. It hasn't affected our family life at all, I'm looking at straight As at school. I live with both my parents and my brother, and my parents have always been very happy together. My parents both have good jobs. They both work. My dad works from 8 to 5, my mum from 9 to 6, so my dad gets in before my mum and he does all the cooking in the house in the week because he's home first. He cooks very good meals as well. My dad does all the shopping too. He goes to Asda every Friday night. He leaves my mum at home, and that again destroys the stereotypical image of the woman cooking and going out shopping because my dad does all of that and we're a very happy, secure family. I can't see my parents ever getting divorced and that's a view I would share. I want to get married and be married for life. I want to stay happy like my parents have been.

I'm proud of my mum for going out and working instead of feeling that she has to stay home and look after us. I think that it's good for women to go out and not to have to worry about it damaging family life, because my family life certainly hasn't been damaged by my mum working at all.

I'm not sure yet what I want to do, but I think that I might go into law. I think that if women want to stay at home and look after their kids, then that's fair enough for them, but that certainly wouldn't be right for me. I think that it's important for mothers to bond with their children in the first few months, but after that I wouldn't want to be stopped from doing exactly what I wanted because of my child. If I had children I'd give as much as I can, but I wouldn't give up my career, because you need that to support the children.

In today's society a woman's role has improved a great deal and women are allowed things which weren't seen as right a long time ago. Women's roles have changed dramatically in the last 30 years. That's especially true with women in the home – they are not seen as the stereotypical woman in the kitchen who looks after the children while the man goes out to work. You've got a lot of women in powerful positions now, like directors and managers. A lot of women, I'd say the majority of women, are out working as well as their husbands and some even earn more than their husbands, and I don't think that that was the case before. Also women are allowed into lots of different jobs now, which maybe would have been frowned on previously, like the police force and working on newspapers and in Parliament, where there was definitely a lack of women before. Now our role has changed and women are just equal to men and doing the same sort of things as men do. It's coming to a balance between men and women. We are beginning to get nearer to equality in the workplace, equality at school and in a lot of other ways women are equal to men.

I think there won't be as much change in the next thirty years as there has been in the last thirty years. But there is still some way to go before women are totally equal to men. I think there's still some men who don't see the need for equality and don't respect women. So maybe we haven't yet achieved what we want. Also I think that mothers, especially single mothers, haven't achieved what they want yet. In workplaces quite a few employers seem to be prejudiced against them because they have children. They are unwilling to make arrangements for that. I think employers should create more facilities for single mums, such as crèches and special allowances which may contradict the whole idea of equality between men and women, but I think that this is one area where women need benefits and need to be treated differently because they are in a special situation that men are hardly ever in.

I don't feel that I've ever been prevented from doing something because I'm a girl. I've always been a very strong-willed person and when people tried to stop me from doing anything I've protested against it and made sure that I was allowed to do exactly what I wanted. But I work in a shop and I often get quite a few looks when I'm carrying around crates of beer and what-have-you. I go to the dump with my boss, and when I'm there I get a lot of looks from men because I'm a girl throwing big cardboard boxes into a massive skip and I feel I might be looked on as the odd one out because of that, but it doesn't bother me at all.

When I was younger I had Barbies and Cabbage Patch dolls and I never had things like Action Man and stuff. When you're a young child you think, Oh boys' toys; and there's definitely a division between what are girls' toys and what are boys' toys, like pink is a girls' colour and blue is a boys' colour, but as you get older you realise that that's nonsense. I think that going to an all-girls school, where you get a mix of all different girls, has given me a lot of confidence to get on with what I do. I go to school, I work, and nothing else affects it. But I do think that there's a lot more pressure on girls to look good than on boys. I definitely feel pressure to be thin, which I'm not going to be. I feel a lot of pressure to be thin and have a certain look and to think that people will only find me attractive if I look like these women. But I have a boyfriend who's open-minded about that. He's the sort of person who accepts me for who I am and that's really cool.

I think it's good that we've finally got a lot of women into Parliament, whereas before it was a more male-dominated thing. Now women are going to be able to represent their views freely without feeling intimidated by men, which they may have done before when it was a male-dominated place. Now I think women are going to be able to bring up issues which are important to women and speak about them more freely. I think that women are interested in the same political issues as men, but maybe some women have stronger views on things like abortion, sex discrimination in the workplace, or the severity of the treatment of people who are accused of raping women. But generally I don't think women have many issues that matter to them that don't matter to men. I think the new Labour MPs will set an example for other women, because now they've seen that they can do it, and they can be successful, it's going to give them a lot more confidence to take the path that they want to, if that's in politics.

(Interviewed by Children's Express)

the personal is still political

Katharine Viner

Lieutenant-Commander Karen Pearce is being quizzed in a court martial about her 'little pink friend', a vibrator given to her by her lover, Lieutenant Colonel Keith Pople.

'This was a very close friend,' says Rhyddian Willis, a lawyer.

'I'm not sure what you're alluding to,' says Pearce.

'Not a close friend in the terms of a platonic friend,' says Willis. 'It was a sexual implement which you enjoyed using, wasn't it?'

'During the course of my relationship with Lieutenant Colonel Pople, that's true, yes,' says Pearce.

'You enjoyed using it and used it many times. You liked to be watched whilst you used it,' says Willis.

'During the course of my relationship with Lieutenant

Colonel Pople, that was one of the things we engaged in,'
says Pearce.

'You liked it, didn't you?' says Willis.

'I achieved an orgasm. Yes, I liked it,' says Pearce.

Welcome to Aldershot, April 1998. No, not the Salem witch
trials or an investigation by the Taliban. The woman under fire
here was a mere witness, called to the court martial of Lieutenant
Colonel Keith Pople, an army officer accused of prejudicing good
order by committing adultery with a subordinate. And yet it was
Lieutenant-Commander Karen Pearce who was drilled, relentlessly and disapprovingly, about her sex life; it was Karen Pearce's
disgraceful admission that she enjoyed sex that was deemed rele-
vant to the case.

Some months earlier, another witch-hunt had been going on in
Catterick, North Yorkshire. The Army gave out a warning that
there was a 'significant health risk to troops' posed by 'at least two'
local women who were infected with HIV. They said they had
proof that these women were 'liberal with their affections' and
therefore they were carriers of a fatal disease. In truth, the women
were not infected with HIV, but in the event this didn't matter.
'I've seen ten squaddies go into that flat at a time. It's like a
NAAFI for sex,' said one neighbour. 'They are nothing but slap-
pers,' said another. 'At the moment,' said a young woman, 'you
only have to wear a short black skirt or dress and you're a marked
woman round here.'[1]

Monica Lewinsky became a marked woman too. Despite the
massive power difference in her relationship with Bill Clinton –
she was a work experience student, he the president of the USA –
publication of the Starr report led to the belief that she was a
predatory tramp because she participated in a little flirting and the
initiation of oral sex. Alan Clark in the London Evening Standard
described her as a 'randy little minx', the Mirror chastised her for

being 'incredibly pushy' and the *Guardian* complained about her lack of 'any moral doubts'. Whatever one thinks of Lewinsky, her story reveals much about the way sexually proactive women are perceived. She was labelled a 'sexual initiator' as if the phrase were a slur.

All of this, of course, is the reverse of what is supposed to be acceptable for women these days. Sex? We *love* it. According to much of what we read in men's and women's magazines, enjoying sex (any time! any place! any way he wants it!) is not bad, or shameful, but compulsory.

Take the May 1998 issue of FHM magazine – a mass-market, centre-shelf men's monthly of the type that has proliferated in recent years. The cover has a picture of a pouting blonde, just in knickers, pressing her naked breasts against a doll-like woman in a bikini. The cover expands and there are six more women on display – all in their underwear. This is an 'Australian babe bonanza'. Inside, there are interviews with said babes, but we're not interested in their jobs (mostly actresses) or who they are but – of course – what they're like in bed. 'His finger went right up you know where, live on air!' says one. 'I'm really bossy in bed. I like to be in control. On top. I love that,' says another. (Well, they're not going to say how they hate sex, are they? Or how an ex-boyfriend pushed them around.) The same magazine has a 'Girlfriend of the Month' slot, where readers are encouraged to 'show off your girlfriend' by encouraging her to – this is getting repetitive – strip to her knickers and tell the world that she's brilliant at blow jobs.

Latest figures of FHM show a circulation of almost 650,000 and a readership of 2.5 million (which is a third of *all* UK men aged 18–34) massively overtaking *Cosmopolitan*, the top-selling young women's monthly.[2]

The 'Australian babes' in their bonanza were trying to launch some sort of a career: but women who are already established are stripping and drooling as if their lives depended on it. (Which, considering the size of their pay cheques before the strip, seems unlikely.) Zoe Ball, top TV and radio presenter, decided to dump her tomboy image by appearing in *Esquire*[3] magazine in skin-tight leather and skyscraper boots. 'I didn't expect her to have a great body, but she did,' said the photographer Bob Carlos Clarke. Helen Baxendale, an actor who got the plum job of a major role in the US sitcom *Friends*, was made-up like a plastic dummy in a different edition of the same magazine.[4] Wearing suspenders, ripped black lace and smeared mascara her beauty was lost, her eyes vacant: the pictures weren't about Helen Baxendale at all, they were about a stylist and photographer taking some woman and turning her into a fantasy of availability.

And then we got Ulrika. The May 1998 issue of *Loaded* featured Ulrika Jonsson, a TV presenter and former weather girl – who we thought had learned a little sense and irony after appearing on *Shooting Stars* – chained up in manacles: 'Turned on, tuned in, chained up.' Her breasts are squashed together, her left nipple is spilling out, her face is an over-made-up vision in blankness. She is hardly recognisable. The accompanying interview shows again how necessary it is to please the boys: 'When I'm 70 I'll probably wish they were still taking photos of my tits.'; 'I do have a lovely pair!'; 'I've got no knickers on!'; 'Guys love my arse!'

In the 1970s, when women started to complain about the way they were represented, it was nameless centrefolds who spouted these kinds of sentiments, who appeared desperate to show and tell the world how much they loved sex. Today, it is women who are famous for other things, for, you know, non-sexual things, who strip. You can be a very successful broadcaster, you can host the prestigious Radio One *Breakfast Show*, but you still need to take your clothes off if you're going to impress the lads. It seems to be becoming more and more unacceptable to say anything other than: *Kit off, fine; Manacles, fine; Anything you want, boys.*

This is more an expression of men's power over women than anything *Penthouse* could come up with. Ball, Baxendale and Jonsson are all women who at some point have appealed to other women – they are not Page Three girls, they are tough, and we always thought they were a bit like us. Sisters, for want of a better word. And so, what power it is for the men at the men's magazines to turn women like these – our kind of women – into *their* kind of women. It shows that every woman can be manipulated into a male fantasy figure, and every feminist wants it really. The women, for their part, have shown that male approval is more important to them than female. Ulrika may have arrived at the interview wearing combat trousers, but she ended up in shackles.

The Ulrika story has an unfortunate twist. When she was beaten up by her boyfriend, the footballer Stan Collymore, in a Paris bar just before the 1998 World Cup, the story was greeted with cheers on a particular TV programme and reprobation – for *her* – in the papers. *Fantasy Football* cast a little puppet show depicting their search for someone who could 'really thump the Scandinavians' and suggesting Collymore as the man for the job; the audience hollered in appreciation.[5] Ulrika's fast living, meanwhile – her beer-drinking, stripping, affairs – led to newspaper remarks such as the following, from Jason Cowley in *The Times*: 'If Ulrika Jonsson wants the domestic happiness she claims to seek, why is she acting like a lad?' and 'Will the humiliation of being battered by her boyfriend in a Paris bar finally prompt Ulrika Jonsson to put the brakes on a lifestyle that seems to be hurtling out of control?'[6] Which means, of course, that it was all her own fault; that it's just what happens to women when they dare to behave just a little like men do. Don't try and live the fantasy: you'll get beaten up for it, and then other men will cheer.

Ask Ball, Baxendale and Jonsson why they agreed to appear as 'tarts-u-like' in men's magazines and they might say, why not.

They might say that it makes them feel good about themselves to feel desired, to feel attractive. Indeed, this could be the Girl Power mantra of the late 1990s: *If it feels good, do it*. We have reached a point where, if we say we find something offensive, say we don't like Ulrika in shackles, then we don't understand the spirit of the times; we don't get the joke. And somehow, taking offence, even at something legitimately offensive, has become a 'politically correct' anachronism.

And so we have the absurd reporting of a story about women defacing a poster for 'This is Hardcore', an album by Pulp, which features a lifeless pornographic model on the front. Women scrawled 'demeaning' and 'sexist' over the top of the word 'hardcore'. Journalists Amanda Kelly and Alistair Clay in the *Independent on Sunday* wrote: 'The hostile feelings aroused by the picture . . . are being interpreted by some as a sign that political correctness, thought by many to be a little *passé*, is still alive and kicking.' Thus: people who care about misogynist images – misguided or not – are out of date, and, worse, they are members of a sinister thought police who meet in darkened rooms and call themselves the Politically Correct. The reporters continue: 'Liz Sage, senior account manager at the Poster Publicity advertising agency, said the current trend is towards the daring and prudishness is out of fashion. "Anything goes nowadays," she said. 'It's OK for advertisers to be really *risqué*. Things seem to have gone full circle.'

The code for advertisers these days is that it's acceptable for women to do anything, as long as they're 'in control'. This can have very broad boundaries – a spokesperson for the advertisers behind the Yardleys Stay Fast 'lock-in-colour' advertisements, which featured model Linda Evangelista behind bars and in a padlocked neck chain, claimed that the ads weren't sexist because 'you can tell by the sparkle in her eyes and the smile on her lips that she knows this is all a bit of a laugh'.

But this is what it takes to be acceptable – a woman to say she's 'in control', that the shackles make her feel good. The fact that the 'control' in question rarely translates to other women, and that the 'in control' situations have usually been manipulated by a male sponsor, appears irrelevant.

And faked lust is acceptable, while real female sexuality is not. If women are confused, it's no wonder. Conflicting obligations weigh heavy: as veteran feminist Sheila Rowbotham said, 'People forget there was once definitely a division – either you were a sexy type or a serious type . . . Then, you were a Madonna or a whore, and that made the arguments clearer. The problem now is it seems women have to be a Madonna *and* a whore.'

Germaine Greer, who once believed the route to liberation was via lots of sex, gave a speech at the Melbourne Book Festival in 1997 saying that, for all the talk of 'control', women have lost the right to say *no* to sex. 'In 1968, women had the right to say no, without apology,' she says. 'What they didn't have was the right to say yes. Now they have a duty to say yes to whatever their partners may desire, no holds are barred. Women cannot admit to feeling disgust or to not enjoying the stuff that is going on – not if they want to seem cool, even if they have to take muscle relaxants to do it.'

A case history from a friend I spoke to while discussing this essay – and I think her experience is not an isolated one, you only need to contrast Ulrika trussed up with the Karen Pearce court martial to see that – rather illustrates Greer's point. 'In the last year I have had two one-night stands where I have not been entirely consensual,' she said. 'Well, I consented, but I didn't really want to do it. But I simply couldn't think of a reason why not to do it. These men had seen me be loud and outrageous, heard me talk about sex – somehow to say no just before penetration, which is what I felt like doing, would have been ridiculous, embarrassing. I'd have felt like a prude. I found both incidents rather distressing.'

This woman is twenty-nine, articulate, grown-up. If she couldn't say no, how must it be for a teenager?

Well, this is how it is for a teenager. This is how Janet Holland, a reader in sociology at South Bank University, summarised her findings of a report published in April 1998, called 'The Male in the Head: Young People, Heterosexuality and Power'.[7] 'Young women spoke of having unprotected sex; of not using condoms, even when they were to hand; of making no protest at rape; of accepting violence; of coming under pressure to have unwanted vaginal penetrative intercourse rather than non-penetrative sex.'

This must come as quite a shock to those who thought that women are on top. As the *Observer* commented: 'Girls are out-performing boys in the classroom and are breaking into top jobs. But in the bedroom they are still kept in their place.'[8] Which is another way of saying that the personal is still political. Or that the political still hasn't reached the personal. Because these are truths: girls *are* doing brilliantly at school. Women *are* doing better in the workplace, although the pace of change here is slow. There *are* more women MPs, even if they might disappoint us. In the public sphere, we know what we want: the nuts and bolts of equal pay, equal opportunities, good childcare. It is in the personal sphere that confusion lies.

Women today are led to believe that anything goes: that wearing a frilly dress is reclaiming the right to be feminine, that laughing at sexist jokes is ironic proof of how far we've come, that plastic surgery is fine because it makes you feel good. But try asking for equal pay while wearing a baby-doll frock, or telling everyone how much you enjoy sex (you could end up in court or the papers or local gossip as a 'slapper'), or finding a man who'll stick around to look after your baby (every year more than a quarter of a million men don't).

The personal as the political was never meant to be a prescription of how to live your life. It was never meant to be a rallying cry to shave off your hair and take up with the lady next door. But what it was really meant to do was create an awareness of how our personal lives are ruled by political factors. Of how the fact that women were not economically or politically equal to men meant that their relationships with them were unequal too; that who does the cleaning has a similar political relevance, and source, as who gets the corner office. Of how we won't have equality in the bedroom till we've got it in the boardroom, and vice versa. It gave women and men's relationships a political context. And in an 'anything goes' culture, the teenage girls interviewed by South Bank University show confusion. If they knew and felt that the personal is political, then they might feel allowed to protest at unprotected sex and rape.

The worsening of women's relationships with their bodies is another example of how women's personal lives have not improved with public advances. While women are taking up more and more space in public, young women appear to want to take up less and less space in physical reality. Anorexia has reached what researchers call 'epidemic proportions'; 4 per cent of fifteen-year-old girls have the disease, and most girls have some perception that weight is bad; a quarter of eleven-year-olds are worried that they are fat. While anorexia has been stolen and used as a marketing tool, appropriated for fashion purposes – supermodels starve themselves in order to make themselves look like they have the disease, and horrifically, fashion scouts go recruiting in anorexic hospitals – the association of thinness with achievement is greater than ever. There is pressure on women to be successful in all areas of their lives – academically, socially, in career terms – and being thin gives them an extra edge (an edge of control, of approval). Most women simply do not feel comfortable with their bodies – probably because if they were allowed to do so, it would free them up to concentrate on other things.

And, of course, if you can't get women skinny, you can at least comment on their appearance at every opportunity – as the actor Kate Winslet found to her cost. She put on a few pounds and suddenly she was 'Titanic Kate'; or, as Lynda Lee-Potter wrote about Winslet in the *Daily Mail*: 'Chunky with beefy thighs . . . The reality . . . is that life for girls is more fun if they don't look like all-in wrestlers. Despite Ms Winslet's defiant stand, I predict she'll be at a health farm within weeks, on a diet for months and more alluring and two stone lighter by the summer.'

It's as if it doesn't matter what women do, doesn't matter how successful they are, it all comes down to one thing – how they look. It's almost as if the more successful they are, the bigger the challenge to trivialise them. The reporting of the 1997 Wimbledon tennis tournament is case in point. 'This year, will all the talk be about sex and the singles girls?' asked Alan Frater in the *Daily Mail*.[9] 'The modern tennis player has long been tall enough to model but only now is she glamorous enough, and moreover, not afraid to display, even flaunt, her femininity.' It's as if he'll do anything other than discuss her tennis. And what about this, from *The Times* report by Simon Barnes on Martine Hingis, at the time the best female tennis player in the world, which is worth quoting at length.

> It did not look like the performance of a future champion . . . which is a pity, because everything else about her is really rather splendid . . . If there were indeed any additional weight, it is all disposed in perfectly appropriate places. She wore a little dress, you see, with little slashes of cherry and peppermint. And it was tight in the places where it touched her, which was most places. She was all turned out in her best party frock, in short, and looking a picture.[10]

Lascivious, trivialising, patronising, almost pornographic. It's more Humbert Humbert than anything else. This was a *sports* report. And we're not supposed to get angry about this sort of thing any more? We're supposed to find it funny? Flattering? Even when women don't want to be sexual – when they're out there, doing their job, which for Hingis is playing tennis – men still find a way to sexualise them, and thus make their job seem unimportant.

Meanwhile, the images we see of women, on billboards, in magazines, are more uniform than ever before. You really will not see the hint of a bulge anywhere – that would be too much like real life. You do get Sophie Dahl, but she is seen as something of an oddity, and a gargantuan problem for fashion editors who simply can't get any clothes to fit. (Although the fashion people ought to try to listen to what real women – oh, how the fashionies hate *them!* – say about Sophie Dahl. I know of a woman who wept when she saw her in a magazine, and thought that meant the world might change. It hasn't. And Ms Dahl has since lost the weight with the help of a fitness trainer.)

This uniformity of images, where a size 10 is too big, is a possible reason for the boom in plastic surgery: there are 65,000 cosmetic operations every year in Britain. Indeed the popular 1990s argument that it doesn't matter what you do as long as it makes you feel good and in control has been used to defend a lot of things, but perhaps the most objectionable is the way it's been utilised in order to turn the mutilation of the body – in the name of plastic surgery – into a feminist act.

In 1997 a woman called Jan Breslauer, who claimed to be a 'former teacher of feminist theory at Yale', wrote an article for *Playboy* magazine called 'Stacked Like Me' about why having breast implants made her more of a feminist.[11] The thrust of her 'argument' is summed up in the quote: 'If implants make a woman feel better about herself, why not? . . . You can rail at an imperfect world, or you can go get yourself a great pair of bazongas.' Around the same time British feminist Angela Neustatter had an eye lift and wrote an article in *You* magazine headed 'Even feminists have eye jobs'. 'The personal may be political, but the personal is also personal,' she said. Because plastic surgery made them feel better about themselves, we are asked to conclude that it is therefore an empowering act.

But how can it be empowering, when it is a very specific, uniform, male-defined set of physical attributes you can request when you visit a plastic surgeon? (Ninety-five per cent of plastic surgeons are men, just as 90 per cent of those undergoing surgery are women.) No one ever went to Harley Street in search of a droopier bottom or saggier breasts. And so by going under a knife in order to get the A, B and C that we think men want, we are asking men to like us more, accept us more, and on their terms – just like the women who strip for *Esquire*. Similarly, after years of demanding that women be seen as more than just the physical, as more than just a body, the request for a man to slice you a pair of perter buttocks is reducing yourself to nothing more than the sum of your parts. You cease to be whole.

And it's all very well saying that we should be able to do what we like with our bodies, but how far does this go? How can you defend a woman's right to liposuction but not her right to starve herself? Support her right to a boob job but deny her right to cut herself with razors? We are supposed to say that one form of mutilation is improvement, the other is harm: but the definitions, when implants can leak and skin can go numb, are blurred. If it is self-hatred which makes women want to alter their body shape through anorexia and bulimia, should we not see plastic surgery – and, indeed, diets – in a similar critical light? Surgery has achieved an astonishing level of acceptability, and the reasons for that growth are not encouraging.

But that's Girl Power for you – it is as simplistic as the Spice Girls, whose message rarely gets more complicated than: 'If it feels good, do it!' Suddenly feminism is all about how the individual feels right here, right now, rather than the bigger picture. The idea of doing something for the greater good – or, indeed, because the reasons behind the action might be dangerous or insecure or complex – has become an anachronism. It's almost as if we dare not admit that the personal is political because we know it would make people like us less. Feminism absolutely should be about public changes, and part of its job is to fight for equality in the political, legal and social spheres. But part of the social sphere is relationships, and these must not be neglected: what happens between heterosexual men and women is as crucial to their lives as what's in their pay packet.

And something very interesting is happening between women and men which indicates that rather than live a bad relationship, women are sorting out alternatives.

Perhaps the most important social phenomenon of the 1990s is the increase in the number of women living alone. The Office for National Statistics predicts that by the year 2020 a quarter of all women will be single and out of 3.8 million women in their thirties, almost a million will be single or divorced.[12] First-time marriages have halved while divorces have trebled. Women living alone, or without a partner, the social template for women in the future. This affects single mothers as much as anyone else. Between 1990 and 1995 alone, the estimated number of single parent families leapt by 27 per cent – and it is usually the woman left holding the baby. Often, this is because the men leave. Nearly half of fathers have no contact whatsoever with their children after a relationship has ended. But, increasingly, it is the mother who appears to want to keep the father out of it. 'I just wanted a baby,' says an 18-year-old I spoke to who used to work as a cashier in Superdrug. 'I liked Andy, he was a laugh, but I didn't want him to hang around, cluttering up the place!' She laughs.

In addition, there is a growing trend for women not to name

the father of their children on the birth certificates: the rate has doubled since the 1970s, and *one in five* women over 30 who give birth does not register the father's name. 'Many women want to keep their child for themselves because they want to make the decisions and take the responsibility,' said Jane Ribbens, director of the Centre for Family and Household Research, in response to the figures, which were reported in October 1997. 'They want to keep the fathers out of it . . . Women are increasingly questioning their attitudes to men as fathers and wonder whether they want them involved with children or not.'[13] And since 1991, fertility clinics in Britain have taken on more than 4,000 women who want to get pregnant and have no male partner. The seventies joke was 'A woman needs a man like a fish needs a bicycle' – suggesting that women don't need men – and here it is, actually happening.

There is more divorce, too – 40 per cent of marriages end up that way – and it is overwhelmingly instigated by the woman, largely on the grounds of unreasonable behaviour and adultery. The women who do marry are settling down later and later; childlessness has doubled in a generation; and the number of women giving birth between the ages of 35 and 39 has leapt a staggering 92 per cent since 1981. Single women are earning more money, doing better at work, delaying children. The proportion of mortgages held solely by women has more than doubled since 1983, now accounting for 17 per cent of all home loans – almost equal to the number held by sole men, which is 20 per cent.

These single women have been categorised as 'Bridget Joneses', after Helen Fielding's novel which has been a publishing sales phenomenon. The Bridget Jones of the title is in her thirties, drinks too much, smokes too much, works in the media and desperately wants a boyfriend. The novel has headed the best-seller lists for months, has sold three-quarters of a million copies, is being made into a film and has spawned a host of novels about single women in their thirties – among them *Straight Talking* by Jane Green (first line: 'I was never meant to be single at thirty') and *Lucy Sullivan Is Getting Married* by Marian Keyes ('Lucy doesn't have a boyfriend . . . Lucy isn't that lucky in love'). The BBC sent out a team to locate 'the real-life Bridget Joneses' and followed it up with an entire week of programmes called *Having It All* and a Bridget Jones night; London's *Evening Standard* ran an article suggesting that '*very* Bridget Jones' has entered the language of the non-fiction 'singletons'.

There is much to be wary of in the Bridget Jones genre – the character is reductive and rather depressing, obsessed with her ridiculously minuscule weight gains, her own shortcomings (she despairs of but glories in her uselessness) and the trivial. It is only one step on from the clichéd female indulgences – shopping, chocolate, face packs – that women are supposed to find thera-peutic and 'female' but nobody actually does. But she is hugely popular – perhaps because many women feel a bit useless them-selves, or perhaps because we're not offered anything else.

But perhaps women also relate to her for more fundamental reasons. For all her jokes about spending half a day e-mailing some loser in accounts, Bridget has a good job. She has her own flat. She is young, she is single and she is attractive and she can't quite believe that she got here and there aren't any men to be part of it. She may seem desperate, but in fact she has a very specific set of criteria of what she looks for in a man and she simply isn't going to compromise. She may flirt with said accounts loser – there's not much sex in her life, so why not – but she's not going to settle for him. She may be searching for a little male approval but she's actually in a very powerful position herself.

And this, I think, is the real reason single women in their thir-ties have been buying *Bridget Jones's Diary* in record numbers. The women I spoke to were aware of being in this position. 'I do want a man,' starts one, 'but if, in order to get one, I need to become a different person, get a less well-paid job, move into someone else's crappy flat when I've enjoyed mine for so long, then I don't see the point.' 'The men I know just go out with younger women,' says another. 'I suppose they're less threatening. But it's taken me a long time to find out what I want, and who I am, and I can't start pretending to be someone else now.' Or, in the words of a third: 'I'm not prepared to give up certain things – like eating.' The tone is regretful, because they always thought they'd have a man in their life; but resigned, because they have so much without him. A woman who chooses to be single and live without a man is making a political decision, consciously or unconsciously, because it's saying that she won't share her life with a man unless he's good enough, or unless, on some level, he accepts her as she is.

This is a more powerful and independent picture than that portrayed by the South Bank statistics on teenage girls. But together they demonstrate the troubling conflict at the heart of many women's lives: young women, having been brought up on the rhetoric of feminism and believing they have a right to most things, have suddenly found out that it's not as simple as that. They might get equal pay, or they might be able to take their employer to a tribunal if they don't. But, at the same time they see reductive, sexualised portrayals of women in magazines, on television and in court. What they haven't got is the right – truly – to be sexual, or the right for their body size to be unimportant, or the right, very often, to an equal sexual relationship. We know these things are real, so why do we deny them? Why are we terrified of the personal being political? Is it that we're so fearful of being called humourless that we don't accept the truth? There was a time, perhaps five, ten years ago, when subverting stereotypes felt like a new and funny concept: we thought, perhaps, that the future of feminism lay in not taking ourselves so seriously any more. It was important to break down miserable clichés of who feminists were, and who they wanted to be. But now there's something wearisome about the way we're supposed to find the ridicule of women so hilarious. I'm sick of Viz's Fat Slags, I'm sick of Ulrika in shackles. It is always men who make the jokes, and it is always women who lose out by them.

To accept that the personal is still political is to be realistic. It is not to say that political changes – equal pay, childcare, welfare support for single mothers – are not important. They are particularly crucial because they are tangible and measurable and economic realities have a massive effect on the whole of our lives. But the personal – body image, intimate relationships, women's portrayal in the media – cannot be ignored, or passed over in case anyone thinks we aren't in on the joke. In many ways the personal is more political than ever, it is more political than when gender roles were more stratified, because there's more up for grabs. It is easy to agree with equal pay for equal work. It is perhaps more difficult to open up to troubling truths about our personal lives, and accept that our actions might have a political grounding.

the thatcher legacy: power feminism and the birth of girl power

Helen Wilkinson

More than any woman, other than my mother, Margaret Thatcher shaped my formative political years. As one of Thatcher's Children, I was just fourteen years old when she took over as Britain's Prime Minister in 1979 and thirty-two when the Conservatives' hold over the future of Britain was finally broken with the election of the first Labour government for eighteen years. My political coming of age began with the election of Britain's first (and only) woman Prime Minister and ended with the image of 101 female Labour MPs on the steps of Church House, about to enter a Parliament that had never known so many women politicians in its history. What did this all mean? What was Thatcher's legacy to me, and to the generation of women who grew up during her reign?

Although I was too young to vote in 1979, I remember the

general election that year as if it were yesterday. It was not the happiest time in my household. Born into a working-class family, and living in North Wales, I was already used to my grandparents and parents organising Labour election campaigns out of the front living-room. So in spite of the knowledge that Margaret Thatcher was our first female Prime Minister, I found little that was inspiring about her politics.

Her policies had a direct impact on my life and the life of my family. For a long time, I held her personally responsible for putting my family under strain. Mike, my dad, was a chemist at Shotton steelworks, the local employer for families in North Wales and the Wirral. He had worked there for ten years, but in the early 1980s faced the grim prospect of long-term unemployment. He struck for about four months before finally opting for voluntary redundancy (afterwards he worked in various part-time service sector jobs, before going on to set up his own successful garage business). I remember feeling a complex mix of pride and shame when my sister and I, along with hundreds of other children of striking families, were given free school dinners at school.

Growing up in this climate, I never believed in 'soft focus' feminism, a feminism which saw its *raison d'être* as getting women into positions of power, without considering their record and policies on women's rights. It seemed to me neither logical nor necessarily desirable to achieve gender parity in Parliament simply with women cast in Margaret Thatcher's image. Politics mattered, more than anything. Indeed, I've always felt a particular debt of gratitude to the outgoing Labour government – because that administration passed equal opportunities legislation and committed itself to full student grants, without which my sister's life and my own could have taken a very different turn.

But as the years have gone by I have often found myself musing on Margaret Thatcher's legacy, to me personally as well as to my generation of women. After all, it was under her government that my sister and I became the first generation of my family to go to university. The statistics and trends tell an equally optimistic story for women generally: a story of female success as women have marched into the work-force in unprecedented numbers – into the professions, into business and into higher education. And of course, in the nineties this optimism has even turned to talk of role reversal, a 'gender switch', as girls outperform boys at school, at university and increasingly at work.

In spite of her own remarkable achievement[1] and in spite of all these indicators of progress, many feminists have found it difficult to embrace Margaret Thatcher and what she came to represent. Indeed it has become the conventional wisdom within some intellectual circles to portray her as positively anti-feminist, both because she was so reluctant to embrace the feminist label and because she did so little to champion the cause of other women, whether by promoting other women politicians or by pursuing policies that benefited women as a group.

This consensus is also a product of the relatively weak tradition of feminist activity within the Conservative party,[2] and conversely a much closer association between feminism and 'progressive', left of centre politics. This contrast has been heightened by the way that the Conservative party has haemorrhaged female support at the polls, most visibly in the last general election when women of all ages turned away from the party, which for most of this century had laid claim to be the 'natural' party of women.

In many ways, I share these reservations. Yet I am also aware that Margaret Thatcher was a feminist (even by her own admission), and that the feminism she espoused fitted neatly within an individualistic liberal political tradition and the tradition of libertarianism within Conservative thought.[3] Her politics were underpinned by the philosophy of free market feminism[4] – the belief that the free market would liberate individuals to succeed, regardless of gender, so long as equal access to education, employment and politics was assured, and a framework of legislation was in place to prevent discrimination. This defined her approach, and also explains much of my own ambivalence to her politics, as well as that of many feminists.

Clearly this emphasis on individual achievement and belief in meritocracy lies in a liberal political tradition that does not easily take into account the effects of structural barriers to equality between men and women and between different groups of women. In retrospect it is clear that some women flourished under free market feminism – especially the more highly educated younger women – while other women, especially poorly educated and older women, have found navigating their futures more difficult. The brand of free market feminism, which Margaret Thatcher personified, created a winner/loser culture and accentuated the differences between women. But as we find ourselves coming to the end of the millennium, it seems to me to be more important than ever to revisit the Thatcher legacy, to approach it with a more balanced mindset, to be honest and generous about her achievements as well as her limitations. We need to ask ourselves whether all that she did really counts for nothing, and whether she should always remain the feminist pariah. For as I look around at my generation of women – strong, confident, assertive, ambitious, driven, some would say quite 'masculine' in our values[5] – it seems increasingly difficult to deny that Margaret Thatcher has had no influence at all. She has been so much a part of our inheritance, and undoubtedly she has affected our choices, our lifestyles and our attitudes to feminism, to politics and to power itself.

Margaret Thatcher had a profound effect on women's psyches and their relationship to power (even among women who were far from being inspired by her politics). As our first woman Prime Minister, she was a pioneer in the truest sense of the word, not least because her own autobiographical writings clearly show that she confronted society's and her own party's prejudices about women in pursuit of a political career. Writing about being short-listed for Dartford in January 1949, she notes

> It was the questions which were likely to cause me trouble. There was a good deal of suspicion of women candidates particularly in what was regarded as a tough industrial seat like Dartford. This was definitely a man's world into which not just angels feared to tread.

That she succeeded, not only in being selected, but in graduating to the highest political office in the UK was a testimony to her own determination in confronting the prejudices and the discrimination she so vividly describes in her autobiography.

The mere fact that she was the first and so far only woman Prime Minister (and only woman leader of a major Western power) is one of her most enduring legacies. We should not under-estimate its impact. In her, we saw a woman who did not shy away from showing how much she loved power, and in turn she made it legitimate for us to love it too. In one stroke, she redrew women's relationship to power, and gave us a road map, a route to follow, a vantage point from which to strike out in a new direction. In that sense she helped to blaze a trail for the women who have subsequently sought to follow in her footsteps and who have taken up leadership roles within local political parties, on councils and increasingly in Parliament.

Whether you loved her politics or hated them, she offered us all a model of female power that was no longer just in the realms of fantasy, but gritty reality. To this day, Margaret Thatcher remains a constant reminder to us all of how much she transformed the prevailing relationship between women and power: how much she upset the natural order of things. I will always remain captivated by the video images of her leaving Downing Street after her

72606

leadership defeat within the Conservative party. The eyes that had once gleamed in a despotic way at the height of her success and power, still glistened, but this time with the tears that were being shed over the loss of the power she held so dear. Although I disliked her politics, I remember empathising with her pain at losing power to the men in her party, and I remember deeply resenting the idea that we were now to return to the good old days of masculine Conservative hegemony. Even now in her retirement, Margaret Thatcher's energy lives on. Shortly after his election victory, Tony Blair invited the woman whose leadership style he has publicly acknowledged he admires to Downing Street to exchange views and ideas with him.

In spite of her historic premiership, many feminists have felt uncomfortable with the idea of Margaret Thatcher as a role model, primarily because of her individualistic ethos and her failure to be a mentor to other women. But the time has come when we should set the record straight and acknowledge that her influence was felt even among women who have been far from inspired by her politics, or indeed her own brand of feminism.

I know this from personal experience. Although my family disliked what she stood for politically, she did nevertheless galvanise my mother into taking political leadership roles – encouraged by my father – first as the chairman (that was the term still used back then) for the local Labour party, then as an elected councillor and finally as the second woman Mayor of our town. This in turn affected my own attitude to politics and to power. As I graduated into adulthood, I always assumed that women had the same right as men to be taking up leadership roles in politics or anywhere else. Indeed, as a teenager, I remember confidently and boldly proclaiming that I wanted to be Prime Minister when I was asked what I planned to do when I grew up.

Her influence on my generation of women more generally is also clear. Not only do we have a Parliament with more young women MPs than ever before, many of these women are at ease with the idea of taking power. The now outlawed women-only lists in many seats may have been more important in actually getting them into Parliament, but it would be churlish to deny the effect that Thatcher's premiership had. The sight of a woman occupying the highest political office in the land created a cultural norm and expectation that women could go as far as they wanted. In this sense, her premiership presaged a cultural shift to power-feminism in the UK, as growing numbers of women threw off the cloak of victimhood and engaged with, and even embraced, power.

For the Conservative party, this aspect of her legacy brings with it a certain irony. Her very success in offering a role model of female achievement encouraged my generation to reject the older Conservative assumption that women should sit quietly in the background, devoting themselves to party fundraising, making tea and cakes (as well as looking after their homes and children) and led them to reject the Conservatives in the polling booths in the general election of 1997.

The ramifications of the dramatic loss of support among women voters in 1997 is leading to a process of modernisation within the Conservative party (potentially as significant as the modernisation process which gave birth to New Labour). Not only is there a recognition among young Conservative writers that the Conservatives need to win back the support of young women in particular, there is also a recognition that they need to strengthen the tradition of conservative feminism, and actively promote the virtues of free market feminism.[6] Right across the political spectrum, feminist ideas are being legitimated and accepted. We are all, it seems, power feminists now.

The fact that she got to the top was crucial to Thatcher's impact. But perhaps even more important was the way she did it and the style with which she did it. Thatcher had a charismatic, ego-driven style of leadership, one more readily associated with men than women. Dubbed the Iron Lady, she often appeared more assertive (some would say more aggressive) and more masculine than many of the male politicians around her. Indeed, it was crucial to her image that she was – as many put it – more of a man than the men she had to fight to get to the top. Her *Spitting Image* puppet illustrates this perfectly. With its pinstripe suit and tie, and a deep husky voice, her puppet brought to life the popular view that Margaret Thatcher was more butch and mannish than other members of the Cabinet. The symbolism was so strong that in one sketch she was portrayed relieving herself at a urinal.

She led with a missionary zeal. Like a modern day Joan of Arc or Boadicea she capitalised on the language and atmosphere of war, whether it was the 'enemy within' (in most cases the unions) or the enemy outside. Here was a female Prime Minister who cultivated a Churchillian air, who visibly enjoyed power and who positively revelled in her reputation as the Iron Lady. She rose to the challenge of the Falklands War (some would say embraced it) and clearly enjoyed being driven around in tanks during the Gulf War in a way that would be hard to imagine either John Major or Tony Blair doing.

Margaret Thatcher's authoritarian leadership style directly contradicted the idea that women are by nature more consensual, more pragmatic, and more at ease with 'weak' styles of leadership and control. It was therefore oddly dissonant with one of the central planks of feminist advocacy in the eighties and nineties, namely the idea that if women were to come to power, their values (feminine values) would civilise society and politics: competition would be replaced by co-operation, strutting egos with sweet reason, as men too would gradually discover their inner feminine selves. Instead, Thatcher showed the world that women had an equal right to be hard, tough and even nasty.

In the way she led, and the way she wielded her power, Margaret Thatcher challenged the complacency of a feminist essentialism which had gained ground in the 1980s. It is important to remember that she ruled Britain at a time when the dominant strands of feminist thought were retreating into arguments about sexual differences and notions of innate male and female qualities. The early 1980s was the time of Greenham Common, the language of hawks and doves, and of feminist campaigns justifying women's increased representation in public life on the basis that they would civilise the political arena by focusing on the human issues of health, education and welfare as well as introducing a more nurturing, more 'feminine' style of governance.

And this is perhaps the deeper reason for so much of the ambivalence and hostility towards her. Her premiership – the style of her politics as well as the substance – so visibly challenged what I call the 'feminist mystique', the myth that woman are by nature fundamentally different to men, more consensual, more pragmatic, and more democratic in their use of power. And precisely because her behaviour undermined these feminist orthodoxies, many of the pioneering feminists – particularly those in their forties and fifties – have preferred to close down debate, to dismiss her as an aberration, an anti-feminist, a traitor to the cause, instead of engaging in a richer, more complex, debate about female leadership styles and women's relationship to power and to each other.

Her premiership has also challenged the feminist movement to recognise the diversity of leadership styles among women, and the diversity of women's values. By so visibly challenging the more complacent arguments advanced by many feminists in the 1980s, Margaret Thatcher has also provided us with an opportunity to reframe the debate about the propensity of women in positions of power and authority to abuse those positions. Through Thatcher's example, we saw a woman who shared a capacity to abuse power as wilfully as men, who was as vulnerable to its corrupting influences as many men have been in her position.

Margaret Thatcher's leadership style is so often seen as masculine, but I would argue that it was actually androgynous. She combined feminine and masculine styles of leadership at different times. During the election campaign of 1979 I remember her playing to the gallery as the prudent housewife – handbag in hand – who understood how important the control of inflation was to families on a budget. This application of traditional femininity was also seen in her private use of power too; she was not afraid to use her feminine wiles and sexuality to manipulate her male colleagues, as Alan Clark's colourful diaries reveal.[7] This was quite a contrast to the image she later developed as the Iron Lady, but both were essential facets of her power and her style of leadership.

In her unwillingness to act out the traditional stereotypes ascribed to women, Margaret Thatcher built on the shifting sands of gender identity at a time when feminists themselves seemed somewhat defensive and fearful of engaging with and exploring the implications of these changes. In the eighties and early nineties the most incisive exploration of the new landscape of gender politics occurred in the realms of fantasy and popular culture. In soap operas and films we saw examples of the profound inversion of gender roles that has begun to develop as women have entered domains traditionally associated with men. Hollywood provided us with a strong series of macho female role models to rival our own Iron Lady, such as the female assassin Nikita; Jamie Lee Curtis in *Blue Steel*; Sigourney Weaver's shaven-headed Ripley in the 'Aliens' series and *Tank Girl*: these were all women who got off on power, aggression and violence in ways traditionally associated with men. So too in films such as *Basic Instinct* and *Disclosure* actresses such as Sharon Stone and Demi Moore played characters who enjoy using their sexuality as a source of power.

For many feminists such movies have not been easy, and have been dismissed all too readily as the product of Hollywood's fever-ish imagination, as evidence of the 'backlash' against women's advance.[8] For traditionalists too these images have been threat-ening, an example of what happens when you let the genie out of the bottle. But movies such as these resonate and reflect changes in attitude and behaviour in society at large, as the power balance between men and women begins to shift and that shift reverber-ates throughout our culture. Naomi Wolf describes this power shift as a genderquake.[9]

In reality, as well as fantasy, male and female values are con-verging. And while feminised man is still a relatively rare breed, masculinised new woman is ever present. Today's young women are more overtly 'masculinised' than previous generations, at ease with 'male' attributes, and enjoying the buzz that comes with ambition, drive and success.[10] Young women are seeking risk and excitement, and taking greater pleasures in overt displays of sexu-ality and are increasingly attached to aggression and violence. They're benefiting from the kick that comes with success in rising serotonin levels as well as suffering from illnesses that were once seen as predominantly male: heart disease among women is rising dramatically, as is alcoholism.[11]

Young women, like their male peers, are at ease with the blur-ring of the gender boundaries, and at ease with the shift to greater androgyny in our culture. Almost a third of women in a survey published by Demos, the independent think-tank, said that they would not mind being born again as man (and the figure rises substantially with young women).[12] My own discussion groups with men and women in their twenties and early thirties confirm that only a minority accept the idea that there are innate differ-ences between male and female managers and leaders. The great majority reject an essentialist analysis of women's qualities.[13] This helps to explain why young women today are on the one hand more feminist in their values and in the way they live their lives than older generations of women, but at the same time ill at ease with the feminist label and the feminist movement's reassertion of sexual difference.[14] Their attitudes have been framed by different experiences from older generations of women – both the more traditional generation for whom feminism came too late, and also the second wave feminist generation.[15]

Of course, many of the women politicians who have followed in Margaret Thatcher's footsteps have chosen a more traditional image, wanting to be the caring sex. They may still want to be more loved than feared, and want to bring more feminine values to bear in the public sphere. And as the number of women politicians now reaches critical mass in Parliament, and as women have proved that they can succeed in masculine terms, it may well be that the time is ripe for that process of feminisation of politics and society to take place. Princess Diana's death seemed to encapsulate a desire among men and women to bring emotions and humanity more to bear into public life; it could be seen as an antidote to the masculine values that have been dominant for so long.

In the book I co-authored with Melanie Howard of The Future Foundation, *Tomorrow's Women*,[16] we predicted that 2010 would signal the end of 'men only' politics, and we described a scenario in which feminine values would become dominant, following a backlash against the masculine values that women like Margaret Thatcher and others have held so dear. But whatever the future holds for tomorrow's women (and indeed tomorrow's men), it is undeniable that Thatcher captured the new terrain of gender politics. Even the Spice Girls, the symbol of nineties girl power, saw fit momentarily to label Mrs T, the first 'Spice Girl', and the inspiration for their own career success.

There can certainly be little doubt that Margaret Thatcher's androgynous style of leadership caught the mood of the generation of women who have been the main beneficiaries of feminism: women, like me, who appreciated what made Madonna, Sigourney Weaver, Sharon Stone, Courtney Love and Skunk Anansie such icons, women who welcome the breaking down of gender stereotypes and who want the opportunity to develop their masculine, as well as their feminine attributes, women who are challenging the 'feminine mystique' so comprehensively analysed by earlier feminist writers such as Betty Friedan,[17] as well as the equally constraining 'feminist mystique' of sexual difference.

And this is perhaps Margaret Thatcher's most important legacy. She was the first Prime Minister to defy traditional stereotypes of how men and women should behave. By showing us that women had the same capacities as men to be assertive, strong and authoritarian in leadership style, she blurred the boundaries between 'masculine' and 'feminine' behaviour and potentially liberated us all (men as well as women) to flirt with our masculine and feminine sides. She stood out like a beacon, as our first truly androgynous politician, at a time when for quite different reasons, both feminists and traditionalists were reasserting the importance of differences between men and women. For that I am enormously grateful.

But Margaret Thatcher's legacy goes beyond cultural politics. Although her political philosophy meant that she was reluctant to champion the cause of women as a group, it is important to recognise that her commitment to free market feminism accelerated economic and social forces which were working to undermine the old sexual contract – loosely defined here as one in which men were to be breadwinners and women to be homemakers.

Her industrial and economic policies – her demolition of union power, her deregulation of the labour market and her willingness to embrace the development of the increasingly flexible and increasingly globalised economy – precipitated and accelerated the shift in power from men to women, from masculine to feminine values, in a way that it would have been hard to imagine Old

Labour's policies having done. And it's arguable that she set the stage for New Labour, as well as the new, more feminised unionism of the nineties.[18]*

The revolution in gender roles would have happened with or without her rule, but she nevertheless was its zealous midwife. She presided over an economy which rapidly 'feminised' itself as men left jobs and as women took them, in the shift from manufacturing to services. Over the last few decades, two million men have disappeared from the work-force,[19] while the proportion of women in the work-force rose from 35 per cent in 1960 to 49 per cent in 1993.[20] According to some estimates women now make up half the work-force and in five years time it is predicted that women will be in the majority, making up 51 per cent of the work-force.[21] By the year 2000, it is expected that women will be taking up to 90 per cent of new jobs as employers look for a more flexible, service-oriented work-force.[22]

There has been a tendency within feminist writing to denigrate this achievement, to see the cup as half empty rather than half full, and to argue that there has been a levelling down rather than a levelling up. The feminist movement is certainly right to emphasise the lack of progress in the boardrooms of Britain. And it is also true that the jobs growth of the 1980s and beyond has been in part-time service sector work, and many of these jobs are not only more insecure than those they have replaced, but are also low-paid.

* Until the 1990s, the trade union movement was vulnerable to the criticism that it was a predominantly male movement which had ignored the needs and interests of working women. With the benefit of hindsight, Margaret Thatcher's legacy was to galvanise the trade union movement into addressing the needs of women workers. The TUC and other unions are making real efforts to feminise their membership base and to address the quality of life issues which women workers have long been interested in, alongside the more traditional pay bargaining agenda.

Those criticisms have some validity. But they only tell part of the story. The shift to the service sector did not just deliver low-paid, part-time and insecure jobs. Professional jobs are growing faster than any other occupational group, and it's predicted that women will fill around 44 per cent of all professional posts by 2001.[23] The jobs growth is in sectors such as interpersonal services, and in retail, marketing and communication, all sectors where women are perceived to have skills in abundance. Women's advance within the professions looks almost irreversible: 52 per cent of new solicitors, 32 per cent of managers and administrators, 34 per cent of health professionals and 27 per cent of buyers, brokers and sales representatives are women.[24] Indeed, there are already more female professionals under thirty-five than over, and more female solicitors under thirty than male.[25]

The 1980s was also the decade of female entrepreneurship and self-employment, with the birth of a DIY culture of self promotion. Women's self-employment rose by 81 per cent compared to 51 per cent for men. Nearly a third of those who set up their own businesses through the Business Start Up scheme were women.[26] Whether women worked inside large corporations or whether they ran their own businesses or were self-employed, 'business feminism' thrived as women showed themselves no longer willing to be cast in the role of victims of discrimination and blocked opportunities. Professional women's networks – such as the Business and Professional Women's Association, the Pepperell Network, the City Women's Network and Forum UK – grew rapidly in the eighties and nineties, partly because of their utilitarian value – helping with careers and networking – but also because of the focused way in which some of them have campaigned against discrimination and professional barriers in particular fields.

But it has not just been highly educated professional women who have benefited from these changes. Other groups of women, especially working-class younger women, have also benefited. The shift to the service sector economy which Margaret Thatcher presided over, and which her policies accelerated, dramatically transformed the power balance in many middle- to low-income households. Over the last few decades, women's earnings have become central to the household income as the proportion of women earning more than their partners rose from one in fifteen in the early 1980s to one in five in 1995, most noticeably among lower socio-economic groups.[27] This has especially been the case in traditional manufacturing areas, in the north of England, Wales and Scotland, where de-industrialisation and the erosion of trade union power combined with the expansion of services rendered many working-class men redundant, while strengthening the economic position of many working-class women.

This process had given working-class women (especially the C1s and C2s) far greater economic independence and autonomy than ever before, a process which has transformed the power dynamics in many low-income households in ways that feminism could only dream of. Feminist values have now been imbibed among many working-class women in ways that the feminist movement alone would have found hard to achieve. (The feminist movement and its ideas have been consistently criticised by working-class women for not focusing on the 'bread and butter' issues that concern the majority of women, and for being overly middle class.)[28]

My research for Demos shows that some of the starkest shifts in attitude and aspiration have occurred among younger women in socio-economic groups C1 and C2. The same research also charted intense frustration at being denied opportunities they feel are rightfully theirs. Many of these women are channelling this anger to achieve change. Articulate and confident young working-class women joined the trade union movement in the 1980s, and have the confidence to make their voices heard. Their confidence has undoubtedly been partly inspired by Margaret Thatcher's example. Indeed, like the professional women who joined professional networks and associations in the eighties and nineties to advance their interests, working-class women have imbibed some of Thatcher's chutzpah and confidence and have begun to challenge the macho culture that has been prevalent within the trade union movement.

Margaret Thatcher's embrace of globalisation, and her deregulation of the labour market, created economic pressures which meant that more and more households began to rely on two earners. Working mothers have increasingly become the norm. Almost half of married or cohabiting mothers with pre-school children work today compared to less than a quarter fifteen years ago, and the proportion of women returning to work in the first year after childbirth has increased dramatically.[29] These trends accelerated rapidly in the 1980s as employment rates among women with children grew more quickly than among childless women. Half of the employment growth for mothers was in full-time work.[30]

Certainly, the rapid increase in the numbers of working mothers has brought new stresses and strains to families, and new challenges which Margaret Thatcher, and free market feminism, have inadequately addressed. The failure to promote family-friendly employment actively undoubtedly heightened economic inequalities, between mothers and child-free women and between richer and poorer mothers. The archetype of the superwoman, encapsulated by women like Nicola Horlick, could only really work for middle-class women on high incomes who were able to buy in the necessary childcare. Working-class women, by contrast, were left to live up to an ideal that few could afford. Still, broadly speaking, women who work after becoming mothers tend to retain greater economic independence than mothers who stay at home, which enables them to exercise greater choice about their lives, and in this revolution Margaret Thatcher played her part. Indeed, the rapid growth in the number of working mothers was attribut-able in large part to the economic policies she pursued.

Overall, women's enhanced economic role has laid the ground for the genderquake, a fundamental shift in power and values between men and women. With greater economic power has come more choice about when to settle down, about when and whether to have children, as well as the freedom to leave unhappy relationships. During the 1980s and 1990s many of these trends appear to have accelerated. Marriage is no longer an economic necessity and women are marrying later,[31] having children later,[32] and are choosing to have fewer of them.[33] More and more are also choosing to remain single[34] and the rate of relationship break-down, inside and outside of marriage, continues to rise with women initiating the majority of divorces.[35]

Rising educational levels have also been critical to women's progress and liberation, and Margaret Thatcher deserves credit in this respect too. Although the Conservative government whittled down support for students by instigating student loans and phasing out student grants there was nevertheless a rapid expansion of higher education under Conservative rule. A third of today's school leavers go on to higher education, as against fewer than one in ten in 1979.[36]*

Young women today are far better educated than previous generations. My analysis for Demos found that while over 90 per cent of women under 25 had some level of academic qualification, nearly half of women aged between 35–55 in 1995 had no aca-demic qualifications at all.[37] Rising educational levels have been

---

* Some have argued that the boom in higher education occurred because many young people had little choice but to go on to higher education because there were so few jobs available in the early 1980s. Even if there is some truth in this, its indirect effect has been almost wholly transformative for women's lives.

absolutely critical to women's progress and liberation, both in giving them greater choices and opportunities and in accelerating the closing of the pay gap between men and women.[38] Its effects on younger generations are extremely tangible both in terms of promotion opportunities and of their pay relative to their male peers.[39] In turn, older generations of women have a greater sense of aspiration, with more and more taking up opportunities in the adult education sector and pursuing what Gail Sheehy, in her book, *New Passages*, calls 'a second adulthood'.[40]

In the current political climate, as Blair's Britain sets about the task of modernising our institutions and developing policies to address the needs of single mothers and working parents for child-care, parental leave, and family-friendly employment, it is easy to forget that the free market policies that Thatcher pursued – her embrace of the global economy and its technologies – were central in transforming the power balance between the sexes.

Margaret Thatcher herself may be less than happy with this legacy. Because, in retrospect, it's clear that her free market feminism was on a collision course with the defining feature of the Thatcher project: her personal crusade to restore Victorian family values. For in spite of her own rhetoric, her deregulation of the labour market irreversibly transformed the gender contract, put family life under unprecedented strain, and did much to weaken the fabric of community life in Britain. As Major's ill-fated Back to Basics campaign highlighted, the world her party was nostalgic for – a society of old maids cycling to communion – belonged to a bygone age, an age destroyed by her economic and industrial policies. And the expansion of higher education under her government did much to radicalise and empower women, and in the process irreversibly undermined the legitimacy of the traditional sexual contract.

The Thatcher legacy ironically put the fire back into a feminist movement which for a time looked as if it was in danger of losing its bearings. In the late 1990s, feminism has a new spring in its step. Fears of a backlash against women's advance appear for the time being at least to have abated. There is less emphasis on asserting women's status as victims and more on how we can use power to achieve change for women.

Margaret Thatcher for her part has the ambiguous personal legacy of being the only woman so far to hold the highest political office in the UK, yet a woman who was positively reluctant to share that power with other women. And of course the greatest irony of all is that the woman who led the party which for most of this century could lay claim to be the natural home of women ended it with fewer women's votes, with fewer women MPs than the previous Parliament and a record of greater inequality between women. In stark contrast New Labour shed its image as the macho party, and has overtly made connections between electoral success and women. The photo opportunity of the 100 women MPs on the steps of Church House was the most potent symbol yet that the force of the 'genderquake' had finally hit Parliamentary politics.

The political environment we now find ourselves in seems so radically different to the one I remember way back in 1979 when Margaret Thatcher took office, that it's easy to forget her legacy. But it's a reflection of her premiership that women on all sides of the political spectrum no longer let themselves be cast in the role of victims and are prepared to embrace power feminism,[41] organising to achieve change whether in unions, professional associations, community groups or political parties. For not only do we have more women MPs than ever before, we also have many young women, women of my generation, whose political coming of age was defined by the experience of seeing our country governed by our first female Prime Minister. Each will doubtless have different stories to tell about her influence on their own lives and their politics. But few, I would think, would deny that

Margaret Thatcher played her part in the revolution of aspirations and ambition and thirst for power that propelled them forward. These women are already breathing new life into our political culture and our institutions. Tomorrow's women already have new blood from which to draw.

why we still need feminism

Oona King

Did you hear the one about the woman who walked from John O'Groats to Land's End with a 6-foot wooden cross strapped to her back? It wasn't a joke. She was 'paying penance for womankind' in 1996 who, she believed, had sinned against God's preordained law of female subservience.

She's not the only one these days to view feminism as an amoral breach of the natural order. The United Kingdom Men's Movement describes feminism as 'the greatest social evil of our time'.[1] It is actively campaigning to abolish the Equal Opportunities Commission and repeal equal rights legislation. In the US, the chairman of the influential Christian Coalition, Pat Robertson, has warned Americans that feminism 'encourages women to leave their husbands, kill their children, practice witchcraft, destroy capitalism and become lesbians'.[2]

Although such critics are easily dismissed as cartoon misogynists, even where such extreme views don't prevail, feminism seems to have lost its appeal. Young women today shun the term, often refusing to describe themselves as feminist even when they embrace feminist principles. So what is it about feminism that inspires, at best, denial, and at worst, fear and loathing? Is it a political movement whose time has passed? Or is it only passé because its goals have been achieved? Even a cursory glance at the position of women in society today suggests neither statement is remotely plausible.

As we approach the millennium it is worth taking stock. Women today make up half the world's population, yet do two-thirds of its work, receive only one-tenth of its income, and own less than 1 per cent of world property.[3] To say that women have achieved equality, even on paper, is to dabble in fiction. Whether in the industrialised North or the developing South, women earn less than men – typically between 50–80 per cent of male earnings here in Britain.

For these reasons it is not surprising that 62 per cent of people living in poverty in Britain today are women. Sixty per cent of people relying on income support to top up low pay to a subsistence level, are women.[4] Among pensioners, 22 per cent of women are on income support, compared with only 9 per cent of men.[5] Around the world, two-thirds of the 960 million illiterate people are women.[6] Seventy per cent of the world's poorest people (defined as those with an income of less than 60p per day) are women. Girls are likely to experience between 3–6 times as much physical abuse as boys. Half of all murdered women are killed by their partners or ex-partners. As Fay Weldon once put it, 'Show me a man having a bad time, and I'll show you a woman having a worse time.'

Women remain a minuscule presence in the establishment – only 3 per cent of company directors are women, and still only one in six MPs. Depressingly, the attitudes of many young women have hardly shifted. Girls are still socialised to perform menial, service-oriented work. In a recent survey of first-year primary-school children, 86 per cent of girls thought that only women should mend clothes.[7] What is shocking, in light of these facts, is the idea that we no longer need feminism.

Like many women of my generation, as a child I took certain tenets of feminism for granted. I had the example of my mother before me – a woman who worked as a teacher and brought me up on her own. Like most of the girls and women around me, I assumed I would make my own way in the world.

For a long time the reality of women's inequality didn't directly affect my own life. I was lucky – my family wasn't poverty-stricken, and I was brought up in a learning environment. I first realised girls were most often portrayed as observers (or airbrushed from the picture entirely) when I was fourteen, in a maths class. Our textbook had the following question: 'If the student cycles at 10 mph, over a distance of 22 miles, how long will she take?' Reading this simple brain-teaser electrified me. I was amazed. It was *a girl* doing something.

I felt proud. Or perhaps what I really felt was included. Whatever emotion it was, it was the first time I had ever felt it. I realised with a sense of awe that boys must feel that all the time. Boys must assume they are included in any action, or that any action is a possibility for them, because they have this recon-firmed in their daily educational narrative. Humans are men unless otherwise stated.

When I worked at the European Parliament in Brussels for five years, I became daily more astounded by the visible absence of women from the decision-making process. Women were simply not present, or present in only the most junior roles. They were not shaping policy, and as a result most policy did not adequately reflect women's interests.

Subsequently I worked as a trade union official for the GMB Union. I represented some of the lowest paid people in Britain – disproportionately women – who had least protection at work, and were often disempowered by policy intended to protect them. The tax system and benefit system were designed to cater for full-time male workers, not part-time women. The problems facing part-time workers reflect the pressures on women (to play many different roles), and the sanctions they incur: job insecurity, low pay, lack of career opportunities and fewer employment rights.

Anyone who shares the desire to reduce inequality and promote opportunity must embrace feminism, since women's inequality, women's poverty and women's lack of opportunity remain painfully obvious. It is for precisely this reason that feminism is often dismissed as an out-of-date irrelevance, or even a social evil.

Feminism poses a threat to the *status quo*. Feminism is the tool which allows us to aggregate our shared experience. It turns anecdotes into economic trends. It illuminates the structural discrimination facing women, not just in our own living-room or office, but across the planet.

Above all it teaches us that in our rapidly changing society, for the sake of women and men – in short, for the sake of humanity – we must sustain the people who sustain the family. It is overwhelmingly women who assume the caring roles, and who are responsible for the early stages of human development. As Ghita Sen, an Indian economist, argues: 'a gender perspective means recognising that women stand at the crossroads between production and reproduction, between economic activity, and the care of human beings, and therefore between economic growth and human development'.[8]

It is at these crossroads that many women find themselves gridlocked. The skewed division of care work remains the single biggest barrier to women's equality.[9] Anyone who thinks the need for feminism will diminish in the next millennium is ignoring trends that increase unpaid care-responsibilities for women (thus decreasing their opportunities in other areas). These trends include privatisation, retrenchment in the state sector, cut-backs in social services, and an increase in the dependent elderly population.

Privatisation often means what its name suggests: where previously the state agreed to share the burden of those least able to care for themselves – e.g. the elderly – that responsibility now increasingly falls upon families to deal with privately. For 'families', read 'women'.[10] Given the division of care work, it is inevitable that an ageing population will disproportionately increase the burden on women.[11] The Government has recognised this fact, and has set up a Royal Commission to examine funding of long-term care for the elderly.

Privatisation, in and of itself, is not necessarily a bad thing, in the same self-evident way that state control, in and of itself, is not necessarily a good thing. However, that said, there is proof that the burden of privatisation pioneered by the Tories under CCT (Compulsory Competitive Tendering) discriminates directly against women.

CCT forced local government to award contracts for services to the lowest bidder, even when the lowest bids were achieved by slashing wages and stamping out employment rights. Women predominate within the sort of service work – such as cleaning and catering – that is contracted out by local government. That is why I tabled legislation in Parliament to enforce equality issues within the contracting process. Although the bill was sunk at its third reading by a millionaire Tory with a grudge, the Government has now incorporated these proposals into its recent white paper on Best Value. It will no longer be legal for councils to award a contract by simply accepting the lowest bid, if that means the company will lower terms and conditions of employment to win the bid. It will spell the end of Compulsory Competitive

Tendering. This is a practical measure that will greatly benefit ordinary women.

Women's labour, when not in the state sector, is concentrated in the informal sector. It is casualised with little scope for collective bargaining or pay protection.

Feminism allows us to draw links, say, between a 50-year-old NHS cleaner in Thornton Heath, Croydon, and a 26-year-old textile worker earning piecework rates in Haiti. Both work for companies that are being privatised or subcontracted out. In the case of the British worker, she is given the choice of voting for a 20 per cent pay cut from £3.10 to £2.48, and loss of 10 days annual holiday, or losing her job.

I speak from experience as I was her trade union representative, and it was my job to advise her. She desperately needed the money. Her husband was unemployed, she had three children, and her family depended on her salary. At fifty she was unlikely to find other employment. I also knew from bitter experience that her supposed 'protection' – the European Acquired Rights (TUPE) Directive – would turn to dust before our eyes. It can always be overruled if the new employer proves an 'economic, technical or organisational' reason for dismissal. In this case although I emphasised her right to strike, I had no choice but to tell her that if she wanted to guarantee her job, she had to vote for a pay cut. In other similar cases where staff refused to sign new terms and conditions of employment they were summarily sacked with no legal redress.[12]

In Haiti, the 26-year-old woman fares even worse. Unions are banned, there is no toilet and no drinking water. She receives only £1.35 per day, sewing shirts for an American corporation whose profits have increased by 610 per cent in the last ten years. It would only cost £2.5m p.a. to raise the basic wage for the corporation's 7,000 Haitian workers, yet it refuses. However, it manages to scrape together an hourly wage for its chief executive of over £6,000.[13]

The links are clear. Across the globe women are doing the lowest paid work, with the least security. Women are hardest hit by privatisation and 'contracting out' (or subcontracting). Ninety-two per cent of the domestic cleaners in Thornton Heath are women, while 95 per cent of the Haitian workers are women. Globalisation has merely served to magnify a phenomenon termed 'the feminisation of poverty'.

In the field of international development, a consensus has emerged – agreed upon by organisations as diverse as the International Monetary Fund, and Oxfam – that discrimination against women is the single most important factor inhibiting development of society as a whole. 'Educate a woman, and you educate a family', is the catch-phrase. It is no less true here in Britain, where 90 per cent of lone parents are women. Over two million children from these families live below the poverty line – boys and girls alike pay the price for depending on a woman who depends on a discriminatory state.

Those who wish to ignore the gender issue find it convenient to abandon feminism, safe in the knowledge that they personally have avoided the female trap of low pay, exploitation or benefits dependency. But even then, there's a catch. From a female perspective you can't 'contract out' your life to another society. Women are still bound by our gender-specific culture. It is highly unlikely that a woman will ever threaten a man with violence, yet women are likely to be threatened with violence by a man. Even if a woman is paid the same as male colleagues for doing work of equal value, she is very unlikely to break the glass ceiling that prevents all but 3 per cent of Britain's senior managers and directors from being women. A woman may chip it, perhaps, but usually at a personal cost.

You will still live in a country, indeed a world, where virtually every important political decision is taken by a man. It is only since becoming a Member of Parliament that I have been able to gauge the true extent of women's invisibility in the decision-making process in Britain. While it is wonderful to think that women MPs have increased from one in ten, to one in six, it is absurd to think that women now enjoy anything remotely approaching political equality.

I regularly attend meetings of twenty-plus people where I am the only woman. I marvel at the fact that had a man been selected in my place (which was nearly the case), all these meetings would continue, and all these decisions would be taken – on topics ranging from good parenting, to new bus routes, to health care provision – without a single woman present.

The same is true in the House of Commons itself, where I often sit in the Chamber without seeing a single woman opposite. This may be unsurprising given that only 8.6 per cent of Conservative and 6.3 per cent of Liberal MPs are women (compared to 24 per cent of Labour MPs). None the less, it comes as a shock that in 1998, so many years after the Suffragettes, the British Parliament often conducts its debates without allowing women to speak. The fact that women are 'technically' allowed to speak is irrelevant if in practice they are barred. During a recent Prime Minister's Question Time there was only one woman in a row of 20 men on the opposition front benches. Looking to the Labour side for encouragement, I noted only two. Although this reinforced my personal prejudice that to be twice as good as the Tories is still to be pretty useless, it demolished the myth that women have made substantive progress in the higher echelons of power. Margaret Thatcher was the exception that proved the rule.

It is impossible to escape the fact that our entire political system is predicated on male values, and that both sexes would benefit from increased feminisation. Nobody, male or female, can argue that the undoubted achievements of feminism – and the widespread acceptance of its principles – means that it can now be put to one side.

As one feminist has argued, 'the facts are not disputed: it is simply a question of how they are received. The contradictory nature of the evidence means feminists can read it either way. It's rather like the half-filled glass, which a pessimist will call half-empty, an optimist half-full. The people deserting feminism are basing their decision on a quantitative assessment that anything more than nothing is enough. As long as they're all right, who gives a toss about the rest? Half-full is plenty – as long as you don't have to share it with anyone else. What we are seeing, therefore, is not the triumph of feminism as such, but the success – and complacent withdrawal – of a single selfish strand.'[14]

When I stood on the steps of Church House in 1997 with 100 other Women Labour MPs, I knew that our presence in Parliament would mean nothing unless we were able to reduce inequality throughout Britain. Central to that work is the attempt to reduce gender inequality. It will be a long journey and we may never see the end of the road, but steps are already being taken by individual female MPs and by the Government as a whole.

One of this Government's most far-reaching reforms, the introduction of the minimum wage, will have a real impact on women's poverty. At the level that is currently being proposed – £3.60 per hour – the minimum wage will pull two million people out of poverty. This is a gender issue, since the majority of the low-paid in Britain are women, and 1.4 million of those affected will be women.

Another vital step the Government must take to change women's lives is to set up a workable childcare strategy. The childcare strategy being planned now owes its existence to the former female Secretary for Social Security, Harriet Harman, and the lobbying power of over 100 women MPs who stood behind her.

We are also seeing the beginning of far-reaching reform in the way that pensions are calculated. Women are more likely to be poor on retirement because it is harder for women to build up a pension in their own right – often because of caring and domestic responsibilities. Legislation is being drafted that will affect these women's lives in the most concrete and practical way, for instance by implementing pension sharing on divorce.

Individual women MPs can also make a difference to the way that other women see Parliament and their access to the decision-making process. That is not to say that we help women because we are women. In my constituency work I try to help those in greatest need, and that means they are often ethnic minorities or women.

Women come into my surgeries who are the sole carer in their families, who live in run-down overcrowded housing, who face language barriers, who suffer poor educational opportunities and lack employment prospects. They remind me, on a daily basis, of the *raison d'être* of this Government: a 'one nation Britain' means nothing unless people facing these levels of disadvantage are allowed their place at the table. That is why the Government's New Deal programme is so radical – it has taken money from private utilities to redistribute resources and opportunities to those denied them in the past: the long-term unemployed, young people, lone parents, ethnic minorities, and people with disabilities.

Obviously, there is much still for the Government to do. Some problematic decisions have been taken and some of the most important policies remain at the planning stage. But our aim is clear: a significant reduction in poverty, and a significant increase in opportunity. If we do not achieve this, many women will remain disenfranchised and we will have failed. If we do achieve this, this Labour Government will have benefited women and their families enormously and, in doing so, rewritten gender roles for the next millennium.

The shift in women's position within society, and particularly the work-force, has resulted in 'a bloodless revolution of unprecedented magnitude'. For the first time in history, significant numbers of women have achieved an income independent of their husbands, fathers, or the state. But as I have outlined, for many women little has changed. As a group, women remain impoverished and exploited.

If feminism is an ideology – and, like most 'isms', it is – then it has a world-view, a set of principles which translate into objectives, and certain prescribed strategies for achieving them. At root, feminism is the belief that life-chances should not be limited by gender; that women should not have fewer rights or benefits than men – whether legal, political, social or economic – simply because they are women and not men.

These basic tenets have underpinned both 'first-wave' and 'second-wave feminism'. The latter, crudely put, resulted from the dawning realisation that the quality in theory secured by first-wave feminists, such as the vote and legal enfranchisement, did not spell equality in practice.[15] Feminist critiques had to look beyond the confines of a system which not only institutionalised gender discrimination, but relied on it.

A subsequent tension arose between 'equality' feminism and 'difference' feminism. The first asserted that women were basically the same as men, and would therefore achieve their true potential if allowed to compete on equal terms with men. The second argued that due to the different roles women played – in particular their caring roles – women were not the same as men, and therefore should not accept 'equality' on male terms, which simply boiled down to working twice as hard as men and enduring a 'double burden'. Difference feminism argued that rather than encourage women to be more like men, society itself needed to be 'feminised'. An oft repeated slogan was 'Women who strive to be equal to men lack ambition'.[16]

What followed was the radical sixties, the separatist seventies, the backlash eighties and the androgynous nineties. The 'androgynous' nineties might loosely be described as pro-female but anti-feminist. This attitude is striking for its prevalence among women of all ages. According to Camille Paglia, the rot set in the seventies, when feminism became 'anti-everything – humourless, anti-sex, anti-art and anti-men'. This perception was wildly hyped by the media who took delight in constructing the myth of the avenging, bra-burning, politically correct, crazed lesbian/feminist (these last two becoming interchangeable terms of derision for putative men-haters). The man-hating feminist was a huge hit. Women bought it in equal numbers to men.

The new feminism must broker a compromise between 'difference' feminism and 'equality' feminism. The modern woman sees truth in both. Equality feminism champions a woman's right – and ability – to compete on the same terms as men in a man's world. Difference feminism argues that the man's world is innately incapable of offering women real equality of opportunity. Instead of women changing to suit the rules, difference feminism believes the rules should change to suit women. The fact is that these rule changes would also suit any enlightened man.

I am personally and professionally indebted to equality feminism, the triumphs of which allow me to participate in the decision-making process. However, rights on paper for the majority of women mean nothing in practice. The dawning of the third millennium will be no different than its two predecessors: women remain second-class citizens, and will continue to be so until their rights are underscored by a more fundamental transformation of the system itself. In practical terms that means a government childcare strategy, reform of pensions, a higher minimum wage, and tax benefit reforms.

We must move beyond sterile academic arguments, and look to the task at hand: how to reduce women's poverty and inequality, without prescribing women's personal freedoms or aspirations. The personal is indisputably political, but the 'personal' in the context of today's women's movement cannot be a reductionist argument about whether feminists wear lipstick. Instead it must give voice to the myriad different lives of women who still face common barriers in their living-rooms and in their offices.

The working mother, the career woman, and the housewife all need to make their peace and recognise their common cause. After all, each faces social stigmatism that a man wouldn't, whether for being 'just a housewife', or failing to be 'a real woman' (i.e. mother), or for abandoning 'home alone' children. Moreover, the economic penalties they face will often be as great, if not greater, than the social ones. The vast majority of British women play each of these three roles, however briefly, at some point in their lives.[17]

Similarly, men do not 'have it all' either. Many realise that they want greater involvement in traditional female 'caring' roles: most men today want paternity leave when their child is born. They hope to spend more time with their families and less time at work. It's a truism that no one on their deathbed ever looked back over their life and said, 'I wish I'd spent more time in the office.'

Other men, particularly unskilled men facing high levels of unemployment, confront an identity crisis of massive proportions. As Clive Soley MP once said: are they hunter-gatherers or parents? Feminism must be about reducing the unrealistic and limiting roles for men as well as women.

The new feminism must validate and incorporate careerism and parenthood (whether motherhood or fatherhood) without denigrating either. The 'new feminism' is certainly new: it represents the desire for a new humanism and as such it explicitly offers something to men as well as women. There is much to be optimistic about. It is men (and particularly boys), not just women, who stand to gain from a new social settlement. Men must be more integrated into family caring roles, and given greater rights in this area, just as women are more integrated into the labour market and given greater rights in this area. As working hours increase for those with a job, and as stress related illnesses treble, the new feminism speaks to men as much as women.

If feminism is no longer necessary, then either its world-view is now considered mistaken and its objectives worthless, or its objectives have been achieved and it retains only historical interest. Neither is the case. We need feminism now more than ever, to cast off the gender strait-jackets that cripple both sexes.

The woman who walks from one end of Britain to the other with a cross on her back, does to some extent represent the true position of women, but not in the way she thinks. Feminism has provoked such a fierce backlash because it seeks nothing less than a shift in global power and a sea-change in social responsibility. That is why it inspires, at best, denial, and at worst, fear and loathing. The feminist movement now faces an acid test: can it bury the warring factions of the past and feminise society to benefit all humanity? The stakes are high. But so are the potential gains.

you go, girl! – young women say there's no holding back

Julia Press (18 years old)

My family is me and my mum and we live in Southgate, London. My dad lives in Potters Bar and my parents are divorced. My dad used to be a housefather. He was sort of a semi-housefather because he still had his office at home. But he looked after the house as well as anything to do with meals and so on, because my mum was working. Now my mum and I – we're more like flatmates than mother and daughter. We're both equal. I get a say in what happens in our house. My father used to do everything around the house – cleaning, cooking, shopping – while my mother was study-ing for her masters degree. That influenced me. I've always felt that men and women should be equal in the house, and that proved to me that that can happen. I don't think if mothers work their kids are disadvantaged. Because my mum goes out to work and all my friends' mums, almost every person I know, goes out to work, and all their kids are fine.

I do want to get married. I never used to but now I do. I didn't want to before because I saw my parents and I didn't want to make the same mistake as they had. But now I see lots of other people who've got two parents and their families work. I lived with a friend for two weeks and saw their family and they were fine, so I can see that it works. It just so happened that my parents were wrong for each other and that's why they're divorced. Then, there was pressure to get married early, but now nobody's in a hurry to get married. I hope I never get divorced. Because I know the trauma it means, and I know, especially for the children, it's horrible.

I've always felt that my career is important to me. I've always had ideas about what I wanted to do – I used to want to be an engineer, and at one stage I wanted to be a rabbi – and they were often stereotypically male jobs. But that didn't bother me. And I'd like to have two or three children. They'll be able to do what they want within reason. We'd never say, 'Right, we're doing this, we're doing that.' We'd say, 'We'd like to do this – but if you don't, okay.' I'd give them the choice. And I'd never smack my children. If they do something wrong. I'd talk them through it, rather than shout at them. I don't want having children to stop my career, because my career's quite important to me. Hopefully by then there will be crèches at work and stuff. And hopefully my husband will have input. I don't expect to be the person who's going to look after the children all the time. No. It takes two parents to make a child. It has to take two parents to look after a child.

And I think if a woman wants an abortion, the father should have a say. Because it took two to make the baby in the first place, it should take two to decide on the fate of the child. Men have feelings too and you're talking about a child, you're not talking about a plaything, you know, and one person can't make up their mind just like that.

I've always cared about my appearance. I was really fat when I was little and I wanted to be thin so that I could be like all my friends, or the people who were bullying me. Now, I want to be thin because I want to be like my friends and I want to please myself and be able to buy clothes that fit me properly. So that one issue still concerns me, but in different ways.

I was bullied because I was fat. I was in primary school at the time and they used to call me names and I once got beaten up after school and I was continually taunted and I never used to want to do PE. I used to hide and I used to go into the toilets and ended up hitting a teacher. I was suspended for it and the teachers wouldn't admit that there was a problem and it went on for years. I had to have a child minder and the child minder was the mother of one of my bullies and his friend always came over, who was one of the worst bullies. I had to spend every afternoon with these two boys that I really hated. It was the worst four years of my life. The other people in my class were all really skinny and all really pretty, and I wasn't. And whenever you watch kids' programmes, or schools' programmes, there are always bright little people, slim people. If you saw large people they were different in some way.

I would definitely call myself a feminist. Feminism is about trying to get women equality with men. Feminism is about women being independent. Because for so long women have been the underclass. I remember my mother talking to me about feminism, and I gradually developed my own ideas too; I've been doing sociology A level, and learning about different types of feminism and things like how the higher divorce rate is partly instigated by women, it's about women standing up for themselves more.

But I do actually think that even if we get equality the traditional ideas about body image won't change. People will still feel that if they want to fit in they will have to be thin. I really think that that isn't going to change.

I'm a Reform Jew, and in Reform, men and women sit together, but in the synagogue where my mum works they're a cross between Reform and Orthodox. The men and women sit together but women don't wear tallith [prayer shawl] and kipar [skull-cap]. When my mum prays at that synagogue she makes a point of wearing tallith and kipar because that's what she does. There is such a stigma about it, the women will look at you and the men will look at you, like what in hell are you doing? I can't understand it. Nothing in the Bible or the Torah [book of law] says that women can't do it. In Orthodox Judaism women are so much lower than men. The men lead the prayer, they're the rabbis. On a Friday the men go to synagogue and the women cook dinner. The men come home from synagogue. They all eat dinner. The women tidy up. On Saturday they all go to synagogue, and the women will still be expected to prepare dinner and everything and tidy up and everything.

The other day my friend and I were just chatting and she said that if she had to be a housewife she wouldn't mind it and I really couldn't understand that, because I would never ever want to be a housewife, because it's like buying into the idea that men are dominant because you're working for them. For me the whole point of having a career and studying is that it means so much to me that women have fought to get the vote and things – and why should we stop now?

Feminism is still important. We have not achieved what we want. There are so many prejudices. There are so many things that people take for granted as being women's things or whatever. It bothers me when people still make assumptions to do with your gender. I like martini and lemonade and people say to me, 'Oh you can't drink that, that's a lady's drink.' And then they say, when I like Guinness, 'Oh you can't drink Guinness, that's a man's drink.'

Taste-buds don't come in genders. Just let people be who they are. I read something in a magazine last month about how sports-women earn about half or less than sportsmen. It's a real shame. I don't think it has to be like that. I think people should wake up and realise we're going into the new century, that we can't be so traditional.

But I think there's more of a stigma attached to boys doing things that are labelled as girls'. Because girls now can easily go out and do boys' things, and nobody will worry about it, they'll just be accused of being a tomboy. But with boys, it's like, 'Oh you're gay', or whatever. At my old school we were trying to get the girls to be allowed to wear trousers for ages. We had to wear these ter-rible tights. In the end the girls got trousers and stuff. But, you know, why don't boys wear skirts – it's the same principle. I'd rather be a girl than a boy. Boys have to do all the horrible sports and stuff, even if they don't want to. I can sit and do things on my own, and boys feel they always have to be out doing things. And girls can be more caring – more able to empathise. Maybe boys are like that, but they don't show it. That can be quite bad, because if you don't know how to express your feelings, it can build up inside you until you are really full – it has to go out somewhere.

Margaret Thatcher is a problem, because people don't like her and our parents criticise her. But if you think about it in the sense that she was a woman Prime Minister, she's impressive, not inspir-ing, but impressive. She's made a real impression. And now I think Mo Mowlam is a big influence. She is really revolutionary. She's willing to stand up for things regardless of how she looks. She's not into her own image, she just gets things done.

I really want equality. But I don't think we have to have things like a Minister for Women. I don't like separatism. If women really, really want things to happen, they will happen. You know, if you're persistent about something, something will happen. If the younger generation feels it's important, we'll make the change. I know I will. Even if it's one individual at a time, there'll still be change. It might be a domino effect. Each person makes an impact on to somebody else and then that will make an impact on someone else and so on and so on. It will be a big effect in the long run, and each individual person has made their little mark, which has made a bigger thing.

(Interviewed by Children's Express)

never give up

Julie Bindel

One evening in the 1980s, during dinner with feminist friends, I declared: 'This phase of feminism is surely dead, we'll have to wait for the next wave.' After the heady days of the early Women's Liberation Movement, disillusionment had set in. Within the movement itself identity politics – which I see as individuals using their identity to silence and instil fear in others rather than fighting for change – had taken hold. While outside the movement the idea that we had reached 'post-feminism' made it hard for us to move forwards. Additionally, the sheer burn-out of some old hacks did not bode well for those of us left behind. When I made my sad prophecy, nobody disagreed.

But just two years later, I was standing on the steps of the Court of Appeal alongside 100 other women from many walks of life, chanting 'Free Sara Thornton' and 'Self-defence is no offence'.

The national media flanked the demonstration, passers-by gave waves of support, and soon afterwards Sara Thornton won her appeal against her conviction for the murder of her violent husband. It felt as if the worst was over and we'd come home. What was to follow, and continues to this day, is a re-emergence of feminism that is a more inclusive, realistic and positive version of the earlier days. Although things have disappeared that we will miss, feminism, in many ways, has never been healthier.

My own journey into feminist activism took me from being a teenager living on a working-class housing estate in the north-east of England all the way to setting up Justice For Women, the organisation that campaigns on behalf of women who kill their violent partners. I did not come across the women's liberation movement by chance. Although when I was a teenager in the mid-seventies the movement was reaching its peak, it wasn't having much effect on the culture in which I lived. For my mother and women like her life went on the same. While women in dungarees wearing women's symbols on their earrings debated whether heterosexuality was bad for women, my mother cleaned up after her sons and husband, got up at 5.30 when Dad was on the early shift to make his sandwiches, and went to work at the local shop.

From a very young age I was aware of what was and was not 'fair'. I did not consider it fair that I ended up cooking for my brothers and father when my mother was at work, or that my younger brother was allowed out later than I was. I remember being fascinated, at the age of twelve, by the suffragette characters in the television series 'Shoulder to Shoulder', even though they came from a completely different time and social class. One scene in the series is set at Conway Hall in London. The main characters are addressing a meeting, calling for 'votes for women – chastity for men'. The audience of women are cheering and clapping, the speakers rousing and angry. I wanted to be one of those up on the stage. I used to fantasise about making a speech in front of hundreds of women. I was also aware at that time that boys were of no interest to me, and that it was my cookery teacher whom I dreamt about at night.

When I was fifteen I found a copy of *Gay News* and rang a number that led me to my first Campaign for Homosexual Equality meeting. The only other woman in the group gave me her copy of *Spare Rib* to read. I was bowled over by the blatant discussion of lesbianism, but less thrilled by the 'step-by-step guide to examine your cervix in a group'. Hard as it must have been for her, my mother allowed me to leave home as soon as I was sixteen. I was literally moving away to be a lesbian. Mum knew that if I'd stayed I would end up like everyone else. Married to a boy off the estate who had no prospects, with three children and health problems, going out once a week to the bingo or the social club, looking forty when I was twenty-five. She knew there was more out there for me, and I knew that, whatever it was, feminism would lead me to it.

In 1979 at the age of seventeen I arrived in Leeds. I didn't realise then that it was one of the nerve centres of the Women's Movement. My first stop was the radical bookshop, where I noticed a leaflet for a meeting of a group called Women Against Violence Against Women. I was terrified. I arrived at an old terraced house, rang the bell and was invited in by a woman in her thirties smoking a roll-up and wearing a caftan. Walking past the bikes in the hall into an incredibly scruffy room, I was greeted by a muted 'hello' or two, but mainly with suspicious glances. I was given a cup of herb tea which tasted like hell, was grilled about who I was, and did not understand a word that was being said. This was to be the flavour of my induction into radical feminism.

I was to learn a very hard lesson in class and culture. The only person who could have walked into that group and not felt alienated would have been a middle-class, educated woman with some experience of left politics. Everything was hard. I remember once being invited to a member of the group's house for dinner. The food was a nightmare and left me gagging for a spam sandwich. When I asked if she had any tomato ketchup she looked at me as if I'd been caught having sex with a man under her table. It seemed that everyone except me had read feminist theory. Having had barely any formal education, the thought of ploughing through a feminist text was terrifying. I went to a bookshop and bought Andrea Dworkin's *Pornography: Men Possessing Women* and read the first and last page. I did this with many similar books until one day I realised I could actually read one and understand it. This process took about three years.

To sort the wood from the trees, for a woman to qualify as 'our sort' of feminist she had to be a lesbian, a separatist, to believe men were the enemy, to dress in a way that would have you thrown out of a hostel for the homeless and not to eat meat. It was hard to pass the test. This particular subculture had rigid rules. If you read a book, it had to be feminist theory, if you drank alcohol it had to be pints of real ale, if you ate out it had to be vegetarian curry, if you used transport it had to be a bike, if you bought clothes they had to be second-hand men's clothes, if you had a child it had to be reared collectively, and if you had sexual relationships you had to be non-monogamous and lesbian and everyone involved had to feel fine about it.

During my 'induction' into the movement Peter Sutcliffe was on the loose, and we organised Reclaim the Night marches in protest of his actions and police inadequacy. We also protested against pornography because it gave men permission to view women as sexually available objects. We used imaginative campaigning strategies to get our point across. Whereas now we have government funded Zero Tolerance campaigns with posters on billboards, then we used to go out in the dead of the night and graffiti buildings. During the time of Sutcliffe's reign of terror, West Yorkshire police declared a curfew on women. 'Do not go out at night alone' they advised. We weren't having that. Some local feminists designed some posters with a forged West Yorkshire police logo, declaring that all men had to be indoors by 7 p.m. each night, and if they were found on the streets later than that they would be arrested. Before the poster scam was rumbled the streets were pretty deserted. In the struggle against pornography many imaginative tactics were used. One group placed an advertisement in *Penthouse* magazine 'Ladies soiled underwear for sale'. The money that came flooding in from men was used to fund a big anti-violence against women conference.

Much of the radical feminist campaigning agenda in those days was against pornography and rape. We developed a critique of heterosexuality which roughly translated into 'Men are the enemy, women are our sisters, and heterosexuality is bad for women'. This was not the case with socialist feminists, with whom we largely disagreed on the sexual politics front. They mainly campaigned on issues of equal pay and childcare and paid little, if any, attention to sexual politics.

Many of us who focused on issues such as pornography were uninterested in domestic violence. We were radicals, not liberals, and as lesbian feminists domestic violence was not something that was ever going to affect us. In the early days as activists and campaigners we saw ourselves as outsiders, fighting the establishment. We were always 'women against' something, and saw everyone outside the movement as an enemy. We could not have envisaged how difficult it would be to negotiate and resolve differences between women – the 'sisterhood is global' cliché was much used, but it did not take into account how oppression can make some women horrible, and that so many of those would gravitate towards the movement.

So how has the feminist movement changed? Now, we are

much less reactive. In those days we would monitor the press for particularly horrendous cases of male violence, such as the Ripper murders or a particular rape case where the judge had given a non-custodial sentence, and protest about it. These days we are aware of what needs doing in the longer term, in terms of law reform or support for women, and we set up campaigning strategies before any atrocity occurs.

And the movement itself is less devoted to policing women's personal differences. There was a time when every aspect of one's lifestyle could be scrutinised in order to judge what kind of feminist you were. That didn't just include crucial factors, such as how you treated other women or how you raised your children, but also irrelevant details such as what hairstyle you had, what you ate, or what music you listened to. There was a time when the 'official' music of the movement was Meg Christian, Holly Near and Friggin Little Bits, and I would hide my Pink Floyd and hip hop albums whenever one of the 'sisters' came round, for fear that I would not be taken seriously. I was known for wearing somewhat better clothes than the majority – after all, being a girl from a relatively poor background, I took no pleasure in dressing like the people social services kept tabs on in my old street – and comments would be made about the way I dressed as if I was turning up to meetings in pink tutus and basques. In the early days feminists dressed to make a statement, with cropped hair, jeans, trainers and badges attached to men's shirts or sweatshirts. Now, many of us who have entered the establishment rather than working towards its demise wear suits and carry mobile phones. Indeed, I sometimes bump into old friends in Jigsaw.

Once, the women's movement was resolutely separatist. Now we tend to believe in an autonomous movement, rather than a separatist one. By this I mean that although it is important to have a core group within a campaign that remains women-only, we can link together with other groups which may include men in order to work towards a common goal. This has been made possible by the fact that more and more men are becoming feminist-friendly in a palatable way. And we are also involved in work that aims at changing men's behaviour, not just at confrontation. During the early eighties, many of us involved in anti-violence against women activism were angry enough with men not to be able to contemplate working with them. For me and many of my colleagues, things have moved on. One example of this is my work around prostitution. Together with ex-prostitutes, police officers, community spokespersons and others in Leeds I have set up a re-education scheme for men who kerb-crawl. Rather than go through the court system, where they are, at best, only fined, the idea is that the police will give the men a choice when they are stopped, telling them that they could go to court and perhaps be named in the local paper (by arrangement of my relationship with the local press) or pay to attend a scheme where they will, hopefully, be taught the error of their ways.

The very fact that feminists are now attempting to interfere in the prostitution industry is telling. On occasions in the eighties when I publicly spoke of prostitution as violence against women, I would always be challenged by someone putting across the line that 'It's a choice, a job like any other, who are you to judge?' I would duly keep quiet or concede. After all, what did I know? This was a product of the way that the slogan 'the personal is political' had come to be exploited by some feminists. Now I would not be frightened to speak up and directly challenge those that tell me my opinion does not count, because I have not lived the experience. This emphasis on identity politics could also interfere with women's desire to become involved in activism. When applying to be a volunteer on a Rape Crisis line in the north of England some years ago I was asked 'Have you been raped then?' by a collective member. I wasn't going to tell her whether I had or I hadn't, just that I felt I had considerable skills to offer. I was not invited on to the rota.

Today we work in coalitions and tend to accept that there are a multitude of issues for women, and we do not share all of the same experiences. When issues such as class and race emerged in the women's movement, white and middle-class women were unprepared. The slogan 'sisterhood is global' began to sound empty when we really looked at differences between women. But today feminists tend to gather strength from diversity, and relish the experiences of gaining an insight into the lives of women who suffer other forms of discrimination. We have seen real bridge-building between black and white feminists. The coalition between Justice for Women and Southall Black Sisters during the campaigns to free battered women who kill has resulted in a relationship that is active to this day. Both groups have been able to find enough common ground to work together and have talked through in an open and honest way any potentially damaging difficulties that exist, something that would not have been possible ten years ago.

But perhaps the greatest change that we have seen since the seventies is that feminism is now embedded in our culture. If ever I want to reassure myself that feminism has made a *real* difference to many women's lives, I compare attitudes of women today in my home town to women I knew when I was growing up. Whenever I go home, women of all ages stop me in the street. I'm easy to recognise: the people from Darlington who end up on TV usually grace the 'Do you recognise this identikit picture?' on *Crimewatch*, whereas ever since I founded the organisation Justice for Women in 1990, I've popped up constantly in discussions on violence against women. Women in Darlington love discussing the latest cases they have seen in the media. They tell me what a difference it has made in their lives to have someone *like them* saying things on national TV that directly relate to their lives.

Many say that they have suffered domestic violence, and that hearing or seeing women publicly denouncing violent men has at last given them the strength and confidence they needed to change their lives.

Feminism is no longer a movement; it is an ideology, and you can meet it anywhere. For instance, although we still have a long way to go, we have won many battles in terms of public awareness of violence against women. It is now largely accepted that it is unacceptable for a man to beat his partner. Paul Gascoigne was not the first football star to hit his wife, but the wave of disgust it provoked was unprecedented. The day after his public apology I was the studio guest on a Radio 5 Live phone-in. One of the callers was a man who told me that, although it is not good to hit a woman, sometimes they 'need disciplining'. His comments were noted in a *Guardian* leader, the editor commenting that his words were 'a disgrace'. When Stan Collymore beat up Ulrika Jonsson the *Sun* newspaper urged her to 'leave the violent brute'. Progress indeed.

As feminism has moved into mainstream culture, we have seen a transformation of the relationship between feminism and the media. When I first began campaigning, journalists were seen as an enemy of the cause. One of the first direct actions I was involved in was against the *Yorkshire Evening Post*. They were routinely placing pictures of topless women next to news items on rapes. We conned our way into the building, forced our way into the editor's office, and persuaded him not to do it again. He did not.

Today many of us see the media in a very different light. Without the media, the campaigns to free Sara Thornton, Emma Humphreys and others would have been very different. The media have taken up the issues of violence against women and children in a largely positive way. Most of us are no longer hostile to journalists, but cultivate those we know may be useful. This has resulted in women from all walks of life coming forward to organisations such as Justice for Women and offering to help. In the old days, we ran an exclusive club where membership was only allowed once you had been through rigorous tests of endurance. During the 'date-rape' storyline on *Brookside* a reporter rang the JFW line to ask for a comment on the issues raised. The conversation went like this:

> 'Hello, I'm from the *Daily Mirror*. I'm writing a piece on date-rape for tomorrow's edition and would like a comment from your organisation.'
>
> 'You should be asking Rape Crisis. We don't work around the issue of rape.'
>
> 'Oh, I did. She told me she couldn't give a quote until they had discussed it at their collective meeting next Wednesday.'

Things have certainly changed. I've recently given the Rape Crisis Federation media training and sat on a selection panel to appoint their new Media Worker. One other offshoot of the alliance between some feminists and journalists is that many more columnists and reporters are writing about issues such as violence against women and children. Writers such as Julie Burchill, Suzanne Moore, Linda Grant, Polly Toynbee and others identify themselves as feminists. Whereas the *Guardian* Women's Page used to be considered by myself and my colleagues as the most anti-feminist part of the paper, it has now benefited from the presence of feminist journalists such as Katharine Viner and Libby Brooks. Some male journalists have reported widely on issues affecting women and children, such as Nick Davies, with his excellent in-depth reporting on child abuse and Duncan Campbell, crime correspondent for the *Guardian*, who previously wrote about 'hard crime' such as gangsters offing each other, and then began to report on cases of domestic homicide and violence against women and children. There is no doubt that both have been influenced by radical feminist thinking and action. In other words, feminist activists no longer operate in a vacuum and that is beginning to show.

Radical feminist theory has now become embedded within popular culture. I was employed by *Brookside* during the Jordache storyline as a consultant to the scriptwriters, and many other television dramas have included themes of *women's resistance to* male violence, rather than portraying them as victims. The purism of many feminists, myself included, has been replaced by strategic coalition building. One hilarious moment during the campaign to free Emma Humphreys was standing outside Westminster with members of JFW, the Women's Institute and Southall Black Sisters when Barbara Cartland appeared in front of us all, and asked for a leaflet. Ten years ago I would never have imagined working alongside the Townswomen's Guild and the Women's Institute to draft policy and lobby Parliament on domestic homicide. Such organisations which in the past were deeply suspicious and critical of radical feminists have taken on much of our anti-violence against women agenda.

One idea I cannot accept about feminism now is one that is often touted: that, now that feminism has entered the mainstream, feminist activism is dead. Socialist feminist turned post-modernist Elizabeth Wilson recently declared that:

> Declining feminist activism has meant in practice a shift from struggles to change the world to struggles to change representations. Where once women's groups battled to open a refuge for battered women or a rape crisis centre, they now mount campaigns against *Hustler* and *Penthouse* . . . By far the most visible feminist activity from the late 1980s until now has been that surrounding pornography.

Wilson gets it wrong on several accounts. First, the anti-pornography movement was never simply against *representation* as such, although admittedly, in the late 1970s we had a less sophisticated analysis of the sex industry than we later developed. The protest was largely about the industry itself and how the women in the photographs were prostituted and violated women. Second, the most visible form of feminist activity in recent years has been around domestic violence and spousal homicide, not around pornography. Those of us working around those campaigns including Justice for Women, Southall Black Sisters and Women's Aid achieved unprecedented media coverage and invitations to address public meetings.

Feminist activism is alive and well, and Justice for Women is a heartening example of that. Since it was formed in 1990 it has raised public awareness on the subject of domestic violence and the criminal justice system. Women in droves would attend the demonstrations organised by ourselves and Southall Black Sisters, coming from as far away as Wales and Ireland. Women who heard about it on the radio, who had never been involved in feminism, let alone been on a demonstration, would come along to support our campaigns for the release of battered women who had killed violent men. The campaign highlighted the plight of women victimised by individual men and then the Court, and drew together solutions both for individual women, and for dealing with the sexist and outmoded criminal justice system. It encapsulated both women's ill-treatment at the hands of men, but also the courage, strength and determination of those such as Kiranjit Ahluwalia, Emma Humphreys and Sara Thornton. During the demonstration at the Appeal Court hearing of Emma Humphreys, several women commented to members of JFW that 'if Emma can fight her corner, so can I'. Although Emma had been severely abused all her life by men, she was tough enough to lead a campaign to release her from prison and change the law as a result of her case.

Women were inspired by these individual stories, and the fact that their success would mean success for all women.

It was because JFW used the media as a large part of our campaign that we were able to get the message across to such a large section of the public. Because we achieved such national notoriety it was often assumed that we had a large office space and paid workers. The reality is that we operated, and still do, from the house that I share with two other feminists, and fundraise by organising benefits. We are well off compared with some as we have a separate office, phone and fax, as well as hundreds of members who pay a yearly subscription. It is not because of some old-fashioned, martyred notion that we do not have funding or paid employees, but simply that this way of running a political campaign has proved the most effective. We do not offer counselling or provide a service to women experiencing domestic violence. Our remit is a narrow one. Spousal homicide and law reform, and public education through the media. By purely campaigning we are able to set our own agenda without worrying about keeping to the funder's remit. All of us involved give our time outside paid employment to the campaign. I believe that it is vital that feminists do not count whatever they do as paid work as activism, or we will totally lose our radical edge.

Today a whole new group of women, some of whom were of the 'I'm not a feminist but . . .' brigade are recognising the 'radical chic' of contemporary feminism. It is no longer a movement which is seen to be 'owned' by a hard-line group of women, but an ideology that has been accepted by groups, agencies and organisations nationwide. It is precisely because radical feminism gives a very clear and accessible explanation for women's oppression and the causes of male violence that it has entered popular culture and public consciousness. It is now acceptable for women to criticise openly men's behaviour and not be thought of as a 'man-hater'.

During my phone-ins on Radio 5 Live, there is always one Mr Angry who suggests over the air that to challenge men's behaviour to the extent that I do means I must be a fat and ugly lesbian who cannot get a man. But going on the reaction from the public when this is spouted on air, this attitude is a dying one. Indeed, on 2 February 1998 when I shared the studio with Sir Bernard Ingham on the subject of single mothers, Sir Bernard became so incensed at my perfectly reasonable feminist analysis of the situation that men were ringing in telling him to apologise to me. Poor Sir Bernard was so angry that after ringing my line manager and my vice-chancellor to complain bitterly, he wrote up his dreadful experience at sparring with me in his column in the *Sunday Express*. He complained that the hour we had spent together was 'sheer hell' and that I was an appalling women. 'What a shame' he ranted, 'that these days Parliament is full of neo-Julie Bindels.'[1] I would suggest that ten years ago the scene with Sir Bernard would have been somewhat different. I doubt if he would have taken my views so seriously as almost to need resuscitating on air, or that he would have devoted an entire column to protesting at my 'feminist nonsense'.

So what have we lost in this rapid transformation of feminism? I think we have lost that sense of being involved in an élite movement. Once upon a time we wore our lesbianism like a badge of honour, and a challenge to those heterosexual feminists whom I would not have even classed as feminists because they were 'sleeping with the enemy'. And although we now have a far more inclusive, less judgmental feminism, one thing that has been lost is our enthusiasm for challenging contradictions in the lives of women. While I accept that we often went too far, it was nevertheless invigorating and informative to discuss with heterosexual women how they managed to carry on a sexual relationship with a man while they were denouncing male sexuality within feminist activism.

Although I have much to criticise about the early women's movement, it laid a crucial foundation for social change. Feminists questioned every fundamental issue relating to gender and sexuality, such as romance, sexual practice, monogamy, masculinity and heterosexuality. It gave a space for women to discuss intimate details of their relationships with men and with women and the abuses they had suffered at the hands of men as children and as women. That legacy is an important one, since the testimony of women and children has enabled others to understand the mechanisms and realities of male violence.

In the early 1970s when the refuge movement began it was only a hard-core group of dedicated women who campaigned for change and provided emergency accommodation. Today just about every agency, both public and voluntary, has developed policy and good practice in relation to it. But although it seems that the majority of people accept that men should control their violent behaviour, the same is not true of their sexual behaviour. One thing that has been lost from the early days is the feminist analysis of sexuality. The battle against pornography pretty much died a death in the late eighties when the libertarians adopted the same tactics as those in the US; they put it on their agenda as a 'freedom of speech' issue.

Although I believe our movement today is a much more open and diverse one, there are aspects of the old one I want back. I want more discussion of sexual politics. I want us to hang on to some of our old stroppiness and irreverence. Our clothes may be nicer and our manners milder, but I don't want us to become a load of soft Labour Party women who dare not tell it as it is. I still believe that men are to blame for the oppression of women, and feel very angry with some of them most of the time; I just no longer wear my 'Kill Men Now, Ask Me How' badge.

Although many of us who once spent all our time in the past in scuffles with the police are now in regular meetings with them, we must not lose sight of the bigger picture. Yes, we are now at the stage where we contribute to policy and good practice, but without campaigning and lobbying, we will not see change. Clearly we are living in a very different phase of feminism. We have entered the mainstream. We cannot be marginalised by wider society. We need to use this power. While hanging on to the 'pioneering spirit' of much of the women's movement, we need to be aware that we are the ones who will shape our future destiny. We still need to ask 'What can that future hold?'

Although the label feminism does not hold as much fear for women now, as it did for certain in the seventies and eighties, it is now often seen as an individual identity as opposed to a collective one. Yet the goal of feminism for me is that women should be able to hold on to their individuality but still see themselves as connected to other women. The fear and actuality of male violence is the *only* issue that links *all* women *everywhere*, whatever class, culture, sexuality or ability. We need to recognise that women are oppressed worldwide, and women together can resist and fight back with far more effectiveness than on our own. An end to male violence must be our aim, daunting as it seems. We should be fighting for nothing less than that.

My vision for the future is that we continue to work from within, to influence change at high level, and that we also welcome many more women into the struggle who are willing to get their hands dirty. One day I could be sitting at a meeting with the Government's Women's Unit, the next I'm holding a placard outside the Court of Appeal. No one in the struggle to end male violence is too important or smartly dressed to hold a banner and march. Our tradition, as the chant goes, is struggle, not submission. This is the legacy left for us by those who created and shaped the movement in the seventies and on to the present day. These were primarily radical and revolutionary feminists who lived and breathed a vision of women's true liberation – the liberation from

sexual violence. Let's make sure we pass that on to the next generation. We've paved the way for them, and they've got a
responsibility to those that come after them. Let us all ensure
there will be a women's movement in the next century. There is
still much to be done.

lesbians on horseback

Stephanie Theobald

'You can't deny that men are causing all the destruction and mayhem in the world. Who's doing all that stuff in Algeria? It ain't lesbians on horseback.'
                    Julie Burchill, *The Sunday Times*, 11 January 1998

Bi-curious female, stunning, 20. Good looking boyfriend, 22, seeks pretty bi female, 18–25 for adult fun and friendship. Ring Voicebox 0640 602572
                              Loot, 13/14 February 1998

Much of the entertainment offered up today as lesbian culture is like those salads you get in France when you tell them you're a vegetarian. 'But I don't eat meat,' you remind the waiter as he puts a bed of lettuce glistening with animal fat before you. 'That's not meat,' he shrugs. 'It's bacon.'

This bacon, this near-as-damn-it lesbianism, has been going great guns since 1993 when some glossy pages in a Condé Nast publication gave birth to the phenomenon that became known as lesbian chic. Its kiss-curled head popped up with a *Vanity Fair* cover photographed by Herb Ritts showing Cindy Crawford straddling kd lang in a barber's chair – a male lesbian fantasy in a nut shell. Since then, the media have been on a mission to present lesbianism in a way that has nothing to do with the real thing. I have lost count of the times straight media types have slurred over spritzers in exclusive London clubs that I am very lucky to be a gay woman because it is so fashionable. Pull the other one, I tell them. Mounds of best back lurking under cutesy piles of frisée, more like.

Newspaper articles have appeared on a sporadic basis that bear ever more ludicrous claims about the current state of lesbian lib-eration. A classic piece appeared in the *Evening Standard* in which a straight male writer smirked excitedly about the arrival of the lesbian pink pound. He termed it the 'dyke dollar'. The newspaper did not manage to snap any members of this burgeoning new class of millionaires. All the dykes shown in the illustration were either dead, living straight women or men.[1]

Lesbian chic is merely the market-friendly face of lesbian visi-bility and as such it is absolutely fake. The dominant media have always been uncomfortable with close encounters with real les-bians, but this time around we aren't being vilified as hairy, deviant women on horseback as we were in the bolshy seventies. No, we have now been turned into a bunch of good time showgirls.[2]

Many of the films which surfed on the crest of the wave of les-bian chic specialised in dykes who died, went mad or back to their husbands. Films like *Butterfly Kiss*, *Heavenly Bodies* and *Chasing Amy* (where the director cast his girlfriend as the lesbian who's only a lesbian because she hasn't yet met the right man) are reminiscent of those man-made lesbo porn videos, the ones where the 'lesbians' lick each other's genitals unconvincingly, as if they were sucking lemons. Such phoney representation – focused on lesbians, acted by straight women, directed by straight men – is like a pizza chef trying to make sushi out of fish fingers. Yet surprisingly, straight men are not the only market to have developed a taste for the results. Straight women too are now itching to peek into the relaunched sapphic safari park. It's not hard to see why this should be. After all, compared with the predictable lives most heterosexualised women lead, the new look lesbian appears exciting. Her tantalising aura has led to an offshoot even more tedious than the chic lesbian and even further removed from the howling butch on horseback: the bi-curious female.

The bi-curious female is the wimpy spawn of the chic lesbian. She started littering the lesbian lonely hearts columns of New York's *Village Voice* at the beginning of the nineties. Her arrival in Britain was inevitable and her existence now thrives in straight and lesbian publications alike. In her adverts she uses the words that the *Sun* uses to describe a top notch sexually active woman. She is 'petite', 'busty' and extremely upfront. She usually announces she's looking for 'adult fun and friendship' which seems, at first glance, more promising than the 'cuddly, spiritual, Melissa Etheridge fan' that fills so many lesbian lonely hearts columns.

Like people who say they are apolitical, women like to call themselves bi-curious because it means they don't have to commit to anything. And now that closet women have read in the papers that lesbians are more interested in being out drinking cocktails than they are in being 'out', they are raring for the off. Bisexuality is not a term they'd like to use of themselves. Momentarily, in the 1970s, bisexuals had somewhere to go. They even had a musical genre of their own: it was called Glam Rock. Alas, when Bowie went off the boil and Wings entered the scene, bisexuality became less of a viable option, and today, bisexual has overtones of Janis Joplin and low income. The bi-curious female, on the other hand, wants the advantages of being queer (which, she presumes, means longer orgasms) while retaining the advantages of being straight (hanging with the heterosexual white males who have the real power). The good thing about calling yourself bi-curious is that you don't even have to come out of the closet – you can stay in there and just slip into something more comfortable. But at least the bi-curious female is an improvement on the fag hag of the 1980s. As a bi-curious female you are at least admitting that you are over the drag shows and the second-guessing of gay male desire and are out for some fun of your own.

Still, any 1970s lesbian feminist would call the bi-curious female a scaredy cat who can't make her mind up. She would also point out that straights have not always been so scared to jump feet first into a new sexual pool. In the 1970s, when the rise of the Women's Liberation Movement felt like coming up on E, daring women – straight and queer alike – embraced lesbians not just as ideologically sound and revolutionary, but as sexy too. Lesbians put a whole new spin on the female condition. No man could have expected that such a muddy pot of low money, low rights, low status and a ferocious gender caste system would have put quite such a spring in the step of a whole generation. In the *Sophie Horowitz Story*,[3] Sarah Schulman writes of the early days of lesbian-feminist Utopia: 'One day half the women's movement came out as lesbians. It was like we were all sitting around and the ice cream truck came, and all of a sudden I looked around and everyone ran out for ice cream.' This was lesbians on horseback hey day, when you had to have a shaggy hair cut and an axe and you went around on the rampage saying you wanted to cut men's balls off. And it was cool.

But gradually the straight girls got scared. They were scared off by the media which invested much time in hyping an image of lesbians as fat women who wore dungarees. Daring not to dabble in artifice is a huge transgression in a society where letting yourself go to seed and wearing really bad outfits is strictly a male prerogative.[4] Alas, many women didn't understand that this media tactic is only proof that heterosexuality is not just something you do in bed, it is a political regime whose function is to make women eternally dependent on men, and many women caved in under the pressure.

If the backlash to second wave feminism tried to drag lesbians from their high horses, then lesbian chic has made it okay to get back in the saddle – but only if riders trot round on palominos performing dressage and pouting at the judge with a pair of comely cerise-noir lips. This may be an attractive option to the legions of bi-curious pussy-bumping wannabes who feel that it's okay to fancy a woman if the woman looks like someone that their boyfriend might also go for. I might even be patient about the developing phenomenon of bi-curiosity if I wasn't so irked that its existence is watering down what is essentially an ill-defined, ill-remarked category anyway.

But the very presence of these bi-curious females delesbianises lesbian spaces immediately. When bi-curious women turn up in our bars – sometimes with their straight male friends or boyfriends – lesbians are often turned away. The space is now partly filled with people who have the whole world to go to but who would rather check out the new Bohemian spot. And it is false to believe that the scales have fallen from the eyes of the growing numbers of straights who are trying to crash our bars at the moment. Many of them would never dream of sleeping with members of the same sex; they are just looking for a half decent social life which is denied to so many heterosexuals when they reach thirty.

Take the evening in Holborn recently when I and a group of my dyke friends arrived at the front of a queue at a 'gay' club (read

70 per cent gay men, 20 per cent straight couples and a group of dykes in one corner making some space for themselves). We were interrogated by the (straight) man on the door about our orientation. 'You know this is a gay club,' he said, looking at my big hair and my friend's lipstick. 'Just as well I'm a dyke then,' I said, looking at the snogging male/female couple he had just let in. He shrugged that he couldn't really tell the difference between straight women and gay women whereupon I snapped that he shouldn't be on the door then. As I went in he mumbled to his friend, 'I'm glad they're not chatting me up.' The scary thing is that he would probably later meet a bi-curious 'lesbian' in the queue who, for that night, would decide to be even more hetero-curious.

In the minds of many, bi (-curious or -sexual) has become synonymous with lesbian. In my office recently, a new colleague asked me if I had a boyfriend. When I said that no, I was gay, she replied cheerfully: 'My best friend at school was bisexual and I used to play around with her. We used to snog each other lots at parties. Once we did it and a male TV presenter asked if he could come home and watch.' Another time, in the middle of an interview with a high-profile fashion model for an article which was supposed to be angled on fairy-tale chateaux, ball gowns and boyfriends, the Italian model asked me if I was married. When I replied that I was gay she launched delightedly into a tale of an affair she'd had with a girl in LA. 'But you know,' she said, 'I only like butch women. I don't want to sleep with a woman with big breasts. It'd be like sleeping with my mother!' She giggled and hastily added that I, of course, must never disclose what she had just told me.

Her way of describing the experience was as a jokey anecdote, a rite of passage that every girl who wanted to get on in fashion had to tell. It's just like the way that top models Amber Valetta and Shalom Harlow kiss each other at parties when the paparazzi fail to be seduced by their Manolo Blahnik stilettos. Fashion delights at the female bi-curious category because fashion delights at the exotic. Full-time lesbianism can only ever be a gimmick in the world of fashion. One of Germany's richest women, a lesbian fashion designer, has chosen to remain resolutely schtum about her sexual orientation in interviews, although it is now par for the course for modern gay male fashion designers to refer to their sexual bent.[5] Real McCoy lesbians like the Canadian model Eve Salvail were only popular for a couple of seasons during the brief interval in the early nineties when lesbians became fashionable. Salvail was jettisoned when lesbian chic went off the boil. *Darling, just think of the implications. Put a real lesbian on the catwalk? Would you get the IRA to lead the Orange March?*

Within the core of the lesbian community there is unease surrounding the issue of bisexuality. The title of the 1997 Pride was 'Gay, Lesbian, Bisexual and Transgender Pride'. It almost seemed remiss that straights were not honoured in the title. Subliminally, they obviously felt they were, since 1997 London Pride attracted more heterosexuals than it has ever done before. The message seemed to be that if you had the drugs, the money, and a taste for free music you were automatically united under the rainbow flag. Unfortunately, many of the party-goers failed to contribute to the voluntary entrance fee – presumably under the impression that there was no point now that everyone was united and equal. The Pride organisation subsequently went bankrupt, splintered and Pride 98 was cancelled altogether. Anyone would think that we'd already arrived at the polymorphously perverse utopia that Outrage! activist Peter Tatchell evoked when he wrote about the future of sex as a nirvana when 'queer boys wank men, who fuck straight women, who kiss drag queens, who fist lesbian pussy who rim straight men who suck queer boys'.[6] His article concluded that in a post-homophobic society most people would be open to the possibility of both opposite-sex and same-sex desire and thus would feel no need to label themselves as straight or gay because nobody would give a toss.

Maybe that will be the case if you're a gay man. Gay men have already made it big time. There's the gay fashion Mafia in Paris, gay Soho in London, gays in the military, AIDS – which has laid low thousands of homosexual men while perversely upping their profile several thousand notches. Go to an art opening in New York and among the straight men and the groomed straight women in Miu Miu heels there'll be fifty fags in cashmere and a couple of dykes bitching about the leak in their eighth floor walk-up. Even the biggest wallflower in the office knows, or has a friend who knows, a gay man. She'll get drunk at the Christmas party and tell you how sensitive he is and what a waste it is – expecting you to have some interest in the tale because you're gay too, right?

Lesbians have never had anything like that cultural and social visibility. We have never even had a sacrificial lamb like Oscar Wilde playing for our side. We did succeed in making Queen Victoria's stomach churn at the mere thought of us doing more than holding hands. She felt so queasy that she decided on reflection that we didn't exist at all. This situation has changed little today which is why straight women will talk about their 'girl-friends' when they mean their platonic friends who are women, whereas men know they would be labelled chutney ferrets at the mere mention of going down the pub with their 'boyfriends'. The idea still persists that women are somehow above sex with other women while whenever two or more men gather together they are bound to shag each other within inches of their life.

Make no mistake. Gay stands for male. It is a male idea on to which gay women are grafted. Women adopt the word because it is safe. A gay woman (or if you're really trendy, 'queer woman') is what you call yourself these days if you don't want to scare the horses too much. It's what you call yourself in the lonely hearts columns to make yourself sound stripped clean of all politics and reinforcing the fact that you don't hang around droopy breasted at the Michigan Womyn's Music Festival – as you may imply if you used the word 'lesbian'.

Many women – myself included – sometimes have a problem with the word 'lesbian'. This is not only because it sounds like a remnant from the 1970s. Monique Wittig pointed out that the 'L' word singled you out as neither male nor female but something miles apart. Lesbos can be a dangerous, lonely and underfunded island which decades of the twentieth century have alternately forgotten or colonised with Club Hedonism-type sexual tourism. Unlike the exotic word 'bi-curious', the word 'lesbian' takes us from the safety (and invisibility) of the gay boy's shirt-tails into the glare of a male-run world that uses the 'L' word as an even bigger stick to bring straight women into line than the word 'cunt'.

In the seventies, gay women fought hard for the 'L' word to be incorporated alongside phrases like 'gay politics' or 'gay pride' to remind us – and the world – that we existed too. Gay Pride, the day, has never struck me as being particularly proud-making. After thirty years of activism the world still believes (judging from the type of pictures that are selected for the national press the next day) that gay men are all transvestites and limp-wristed muscle bunnies and that lesbians only exist if they are wearing lipstick. Most newspaper editors are too scared to use pictures of butch women unless they are making a joke about them. But on occasion, listening to Boy George or Ian McKellen on TV – both of whom can usually be relied on to team the word 'gay' up with 'lesbian' when talking about gay and lesbian issues – I feel a slight glow not of pride but of power that I am being included, mentioned, accounted for.

Gay men don't understand this sense of marginality. When they open their lonely hearts columns they are not assailed with a word, 'bi-curious', which expresses more homosexual shame than pride. The money that gay men have invested in their community means that 'gay' has become a brand name as established and cool as Gucci, Absolut or Sony. The popularity of 'Gay' the brand has been helped by having a whole adventure playground of sexuality surrounding it. Bi-curious male? Where's the interest in that when being out and out gay is much sexier? Why beat about the bush when you can go to nightly underwear parties if you live in London and where the gay male press has lonely hearts columns which specialise in categories like 'Meat Rack,' 'Wet and Dirty', 'Fuck Fest' and 'Three or More'?[7]

Not all dykes reject the bi-curious out of hand. Some have the patience for them. Lesbian sex radical Susie Bright writes in her essay 'What Is It About Straight Women?'[8] that many lesbian-dabblers end up jumping the fence in the end. After all, most dykes were straight once. Maybe bi-curious is just a chrysalis stage prior to seeing the light. Bright says that in her experience, 'they'll start making love back to you and come up with all kinds of little tricks that will make your clit jump up and wonder where the time went. All of a sudden, your precious, innocent straight lady will be gone. You'll find yourself with a real, live Sapphic Wonder.'

It's tempting to believe this scenario. Now that bi-curious entreaties are cropping up everywhere – including non-gay publications like *Loot* – it is surprising that nobody is looking into the possibility that the bi-curious female might turn out to be the protagonist of that long-overdue sexuality revolution we've all been promised. Maybe Valerie Solanas' *SCUM Manifesto*[9] is on the verge of coming true. Maybe these pesky sex tourists are the first in a fierce stampede of 'dominant, secure, self-confident, nasty, violent, selfish, independent, proud, thrill-seeking, free-wheeling, arrogant females who consider themselves fit to rule the universe.'

Unfortunately, most of the people who could be generals of the revolution – the country's agony aunts – still sound like they've been reading too much Radclyffe Hall. *Cosmopolitan's* Irma Kurtz is one of the worst. Call up her 'Could You Be Gay?' telephone help line ('one of readers' most common worries') and you think you've stumbled by mistake on to the *Well of Loneliness* fan club. True, Irma never actually says that her bi-curious readers are blemished by the mark of Cain, that though they may be faithful even until death the world will call their love unclean. But in her campy *Cosmo* lingo she pretty much says the same thing. She tells the thousands of women callers worried by recurring dreams of sleeping naked in a single sleeping bag with their blonde personnel manager that the idea (Irma steers clear of the 'L' word) is a dangerous one but that if they must, then they should live a 'conscientious life with dignity'. Living with dignity presumably means that you should not have as much sex as men. But conscientious? Does that mean cleaning your stout walking boots three times a day and ironing your manly breeches afterwards?

The best bit comes when Irma (whose haircut and glasses could be mistaken for pure lesbian circa 1973) tells you that even if you have gone to bed with another women, then all is not lost since: 'a taste for amateur theatricals does not make you a movie star.' That is quite cute. If Irma means that we shag like Marlene Dietrich while the growing legions of bi-curious have the sexual chutzpah of the vicar's wife who keeps forgetting her lines on the opening night of *Snow White*, then she has a point. Most bi-curious women have been sexually brought up by men and have consequently lost much of their capacity to act dirty. A typical date with Ms Bi-Try will involve a monologue about her imperfect body and lamentations about what an asshole her boyfriend is. When you finally lure her back to your pad (and this usually takes a while since Ms Bi-Try seems to believe that The Rules apply to lesbians too) she will lie on her back and expect you to transport her to pleasure mountain. This can be difficult since there are areas of her body that she usually forbids you to venture on. Being in bed with her is like tiptoeing round a minefield feeling that any minute you might stumble over a tripwire which will cause everything to blow up completely. The cunt is the main tripwire. That is no surprise given that these girls have spent their lives shying away from naming their sex organs and becoming embarrassed when their boyfriends use the word as an insult.

Part of me thinks that Irma should be telling the bi-curious to get out there and just do it, even if it is just a short run of Puss in Boots down on Clacton Pier. Come on, life's not that interesting, there aren't that many exciting things to do in the world. In Plato's Cave of heterosexuality, the shadows on the wall may seem pretty exciting – but in the bright world of lesbianism, women kiss better than men, and oral sex is par for the course.

Although I have ambivalent feelings towards the bi-curious female, I do find it strange that Irma and her agony ilk still insist on plugging the supposed joys of heterosexuality. You'd have thought that if heterosexuality was so natural then the man/woman sex dynamic would not have to be propagandised so relentlessly. And the propaganda doesn't just appear in Irma's domain. Read any book, watch any film, flick through any paper and you'll see the vehemence which goes into propping up a supposedly natural system. Last summer, I was commissioned by a friend at *She* magazine to write a piece called 'How to Make Love to a Woman, by a Lesbian'. 'Readers will love it,' she said. 'Make it funny. You know: "Cunnilingus Part 1, 2 and 3." "In the 1980s real men ate quiche, now they eat cunt." That sort of thing.' When I'd written the article everything seemed to be going fine. I was even amused when I learnt that *She* had called an emergency meeting to decide whether the word 'cunt' was suitable for its readership (it wasn't, of course, and was replaced with the altogether less funny 'vagina').

But then things took a turn for the worse. The day before the issue closed I received a call from my friend who told me, in embarrassed tones, that my story had been, well, knobbled. It had been going through the final stages of vetting by a female lawyer. She had loved it. Her staff had loved it. Loved it so much in fact that all the secretaries who worked for her had gone tittering round the office making photocopies so they could take it home to read at their leisure. When one of the head lawyers emerged from his office to see what all the excitement was about, he too was shown a copy.

According to witness accounts, he took it into his office and came out looking pale. No doubt concerned on his client's behalf about tendencies to deprave and corrupt, he claimed that it was in 'bad taste' and sent it immediately to a senior manager who was also shocked. He accused the article of 'advocating lesbianism' and said that W H Smiths would refuse to stock it. He ordered the offending word 'lesbian' to be removed not just from the front cover but also from the main headline inside the magazine and the story was softened up beyond recognition. 'How to Make Love to a Woman, by a Lesbian' became 'Better Sex for Bored Couples.'

'I can't tell you how bad all the women feel at *She*,' my friend sighed later. 'Every man's mag you pick up has got stuff about gay women and sex. It seems that men are allowed to write about lesbians but women aren't.' I sighed too, and sighed again as I reminded myself that most straight women still didn't realise quite how unfashionable their trendy dyke friends are in the eyes of the suits who run the world. On the bright side, maybe the senior manager had a point. Maybe the power of the word 'lesbian' would make *She* readers all over the land dump their husbands and run off with the nanny. It would, after all, only be exacerbating a trend that has been happening for years; first the trickle and then the flood of women who decided to opt out, to come into being and come with women.

Few people have heard of any pre-twentieth century lesbians apart from, maybe, Sappho. Even for much of the twentieth century, identifying yourself as a 100% lesbian has been at best half-hearted, at worst life-threatening. In the Bohemian 1920s[10], lesbians were characterised by bisexual compromise. In the 1930s they were painted as monstrosities in a time of great unemployment when non-nurturing women were freaks of nature. In the 1940s, when the needs-must politics of the war favoured women's independence, 'odd girls' started surfacing like 'foxes from their holes'.[11] Yet, similar to the 1930s backlash, the 1950s came to clamp down heavily on the freedoms gained.

The 1960s brought a spirit of flower power radicalism that hardened into 1970s lesbian politics. For the first time, many women could survive financially without having to marry men or beg their fathers. The eighties were marked by, on the one hand, extreme conservatism and on the other a determination to experiment with lust and banish the image of the hair-stroking, bun-scoffing lesbian – an experiment which succeeded in splintering the so-called community even further. In the early nineties, lesbians got militant. At first they tagged on to Act Up, the men's AIDS-propelled agitprop forum which centred around public 'zaps' like staged kiss-ins and *tableaux vivants* die-ins. Frustration with having to concentrate on gay male issues led to the creation of the Lesbian Avengers whose tongue-in-cheek slogan 'We Recruit' proved an attractive come-on for the hundreds of lesbians who joined various international chapters in the hope of raising lesbian visibility and doing some serious cruising at the same time. When it was founded in 1993 the London chapter grew and grew, as if lesbianism was one of Saatchi's more successful ad campaigns. Lesbians weren't being recruited, they were handing themselves in.

The Lesbian Avengers have now disbanded in London. The big thing currently is to go large at the Candy Bar, the first full-time lesbian bar in the UK which stands in the heart of Soho alongside all the gay boy bars. The ebbing and flowing of lesbian politics and identity seem to have cascaded back to the 1920s when women's bars in New York's Harlem like the Clam House and Connie's Inn attracted homosexuals looking for a place they could feel at home as well as voyeurs up for some exotic thrills before going back to the decent parts of town.

These days, self-promoting rebel rousers might occasionally flash the lesbian card as proof of being true subversives but it is always emphasised as a part-time thing – something wacky like a speed habit or a penchant for SM sex with men. Julie Burchill, for instance, splatters her autobiography *I Knew I Was Right* with hints of sapphic inclinations during the time she worked as a teenage reporter at the NME, but she can never quite bring herself to go the whole way. When Tony Parsons accuses her of being a frigid dyke she marries him. When she finally gets round to having a high-profile affair with Charlotte Raven she again backs off from the whole lesbo label and says that she and Charlotte are simply 'born to be notorious'. It might serve Burchill's purpose to insinuate that all women who sleep with other women are 'notorious', i.e. glue-sniffing, Satan-worshipping sort of girls. But views like this only encourage people to think I get hot pussy action every night in some Medici-style love palace. Nobody stops to consider the reality behind the mask. If my work colleagues ask me, of a Wednesday night, if I am going out and I reply that I am going to a lesbian lap dancing evening (because at last, in 1998 we finally have a place where we get to act like lechy straight men one night of the week),[12] they smile in a satisfied 'that's my girl' sort of way. They seem to think I lead a sexual life of Riley. They don't realise that lesbians come the lowest on the sexuality food chain, that most nights of the week, if you want to hang out with like-minded women, you have to trek to the middle of nowhere to find a dingy bar with 50 per cent dykes, if you're lucky. Or if you don't want to risk life and limb in the middle of nowhere you can go to one of the hundreds of gay men's bars crammed with gay men who eye you scornfully as you enter, as if you're taking up valuable dick space, which, of course, you are. And this is London in the late 1990s.

Stepping from the straight world into the lesbian one can feel weird sometimes. It's a little bit like being in a twisted *The Lion, the Witch and the Wardrobe* where you're always having to step back into the closet and come out the other side in a penny-pinched Narnia. Here, although pockets of girls brandish lipstick and twenty-pound notes, the majority socialise in seedy bars, battle with internalised homophobia and spend much of their time being ground down by their lack of basic rights – the right, for instance, to live with someone you love.

Last year, I attended what could have been – what should have been – the wedding reception of two friends of mine. The location was a dingy room above a pub in London's Islington where all the women were wearing A-line pastel-coloured frocks. The atmosphere was more like a wake than a wedding. When I approached one of my friends, let's call her Nicola, she pointed mournfully over to her 'bride', a short-haired woman in a black Next skirt suit who, at that moment, was attempting to kiss a young man with a Tintin haircut. 'Come on,' the woman taking a photo was saying, 'Do it for a bit longer! We've got a whole album to do yet.'

Nicola met her girlfriend, Susan – the woman in the Next skirt – two years ago in New York. It was nothing unusual. A case of girl meets girl, girl falls in love with girl. After two years of travelling to and from their respective countries, they wanted to make a life together. If they were straight they could have married but they were not, so they had to find a gay man who didn't mind putting on a show for the sake of legalising her life with her real lover. All three of them went through a furtive ceremony that felt like a sexuality Speakeasy,[13] but at least if immigration control ever decided to check up – which they do – then they would have a full set of snapshots and wedding presents to convince them that love was in the air. Like war vets who die alone in rat-infested council flats because they can't afford any heating, the mighty viragos seemed to have fallen. The fearless horsewomen have been reduced to exchanging oaths with gay men and wearing A-line skirts in the name of impersonating straight women. But hey, at least you could call it genuine lesbian entertainment.

My friend Nicola was sanguine about the rise of the bi-curious. Undoubtedly, she said, the image of lesbians had changed of late. They were more body- and clothes-conscious, and politics had been filtered down to politics of fun. She said it was nothing to worry about. It was just the to-ing and fro-ing of sexual politics. The younger generation of lesbians called themselves 'bisexuals' or 'attitude free' while bisexuals now preferred to call themselves bi-curious. Who knows what Nicola and Susan's wedding would have looked like had gay politics continued with the ferocity that it had in the 1970s? I have no desire to get married, but it irritates me that the straight people who pay lip-service to the idea of gay rights still balk at the idea of gays and lesbians getting married or adopting children. If you think we're OK? Then shut up and give us equal rights.

Me, I like to drop my lesbianism like a bomb. It's just more stylish to do it that way because even if you wrap it up in tissue paper and handle it with kid gloves, it's still going to go bang sooner or later. But whatever way you do it, you have to do it. Not just for self-respect but because when your job takes you to sojourn on the shiny side of the Narnia closet you have a duty to highlight life on the other side.

During one Paris fashion week, I had lunch at the Ritz with the publicity director of Valentino. His gayboy badinage was on middling form – 'That foam disco last night! My God, you should have seen the bodies on those boys' – but I could see he was struggling to keep his attention focused on me. Jack Nicolson's ex-wife was holding court at the next table and a creature in Chanel shades and a Pucci headscarf kept waving at him from across the room. Nothing unusual about that. It is the eternal law of the fashion hierarchy that if you are not a gay man – either old and rich or young and beautiful – then you had better be Sharon Stone or the editor of an important glossy magazine. If you are a straight woman fashion writer on a low circulation newspaper that not many people have heard of, you had better be, as Andy Warhol said, either a looker or a talker.

Bored – yet again – of being presumed straight until proved otherwise I decided to talk. 'Actually,' I said, 'I'm not interested in boys. I'm a lesbian and I wouldn't mind trying my luck with Donatella Versace. What do you think of my chances?' The PR man's fork froze above his plate as if his *terrine de lapin* had suddenly gone out of fashion.

But sometimes I feel like a voice crying in the desert. My fantasy scenario spectrum begins with earnest desires, such as lessons for seven-year-olds at primary school about gays and lesbians. It moves through envious reverie, like an economically buoyant lesbian community that would enable me to live like a gayboy, with the option to shag or get shagged for free at three o'clock on a Wednesday afternoon in February if I so fancied it.

But most of all in these days of flabby politics, it strikes me as about time we had a lesbian feminist revival rather than a bi-curiously half-hearted orgy. You might enjoy it too. After all, every straight dinner party I go to these days is filled with professional, high-powered straight girls bemoaning the fact that they don't believe in anything any more. Their topics of conversation include yoga, karma and feng shui. Madonna summed up this general mood of female mardiness in 1998 by declaring she thought that 'people are turning more inwards, going "Who am I? What am I doing?"'[14]

Let me assure all those women who don't know what they're doing that there is nothing like being a minority to keep you on your toes. With lesbian feminism this time around just remember two things: you don't have to sleep with us and if you do, then would you please stick to your guns.

Ladies, your horses await.

lentils and lilies

a story

Helen Simpson

Jade Beaumont was technically up in her bedroom revising for the A-levels which were now only weeks away. Her school gave them study days at home, after lectures on trust and idleness. She was supposed to be sorting out the differences between Wordsworth and Coleridge at the moment.

Down along the suburban pleasantness of Miniver Road the pavements were shaded by fruit trees, and the front gardens of the little Edwardian villas smiled back at her with early lilac, bushes of crimson-flowering currant and the myopic blue dazzle of forget-me-nots. She felt light on her feet and clever, like a cat, snuffing the air, pinching a pungent currant leaf.

There was a belief held by Jade's set that the earlier you hardened yourself off and bared your skin, the more lasting the eventual tan; and so she had that morning pulled on a brief white skirt and T-shirt. She was on her way to an interview for a holiday job at the garden centre. Summer! She couldn't wait. The morning was fair but chilly and the white-gold hairs on her arms and legs stood up and curved to form an invisible reticulation, trapping a layer of warm air a good centimetre deep.

> *I may not hope from outward forms to win*
> *The passion and the life, whose fountains are within.*

That was cool, but Coleridge was a minefield. Just when you thought he'd said something really brilliant, he went raving off full-steam ahead into nothingness. He was a nightmare to write about. Anyway, she herself found outward forms utterly absorbing, the colour of clothes, the texture of skin, the smell of food and flowers. She couldn't see the point of extrapolation. Keats was obviously so much better than the others, but you didn't get the choice of questions with him.

She paused to inhale the sweet air around a *Philadelphus* 'Belle Etoile', then noticed the host of tired daffodils at its feet.

> *Shades of the prison-house begin to close*
> *Upon the growing boy,*
> *But he beholds the light, and whence it flows,*
> *He sees it in his joy.*

She looked back down her years at school, the reined-in feeling, the stupors of boredom, the teachers in the classrooms like tired lion-tamers, and felt quite the opposite. She was about to be let out. And every day when she went out of the house, there was the excitement of being noticed, the warmth of eye-beams, the unfolding consciousness of her own attractive powers. She was the focus of every film she saw, every novel she read. She was about to start careering round like a lustrous loose cannon.

Full soon thy Soul shall have her earthly freight,
And custom lie upon thee with a weight,
Heavy as frost, and deep almost as life

She was never going to go dead inside or live somewhere boring like this, and she would make sure she was in charge of any work she did and not let it run her. She would never be like her mother, making rotas and lists and endless arrangements, lost forever in a forest of twitching detail with her tense talk of juggling and her self-importance about her precious job and her joyless 'running the family'. No, life was not a route march; or, at least, *hers* would not be.

When she thought of her mother, she saw tendons and hawsers, a taut figure at the front door screaming at them all to do their music practice. She was always off out; she made them do what she said by remote control. Her trouble was she'd forgotten how to relax. It was no wonder Dad was like he was.

And everybody said she was so amazing, what she managed to pack into twenty-four hours. Dad worked hard, they said, but she worked hard too *and* did the home shift, whatever that was. Not really so very amazing though; she'd forgotten to get petrol a couple of weeks ago, and the school run had ground to a halt. In fact some people might say downright inefficient.

On the opposite side of the road, a tall girl trailed past with a double buggy of grizzling babies, a Walkman's shrunken tinkling at her ears. Au pair, remarked Jade expertly to herself, scrutinising the girl's shoes, cerise plastic jellies set with glitter. She wanted some just like that, but without the purple edging.

She herself had been dragged up by a string of au pairs. Her mother hated it when she said that. After all, she *was* supposed to take delight in us! thought Jade viciously, standing stock-still, outraged; like, *be* there with us. For us. Fair seed-time had my soul I *don't* think.

Above her the cherry trees were fleecy and packed with a foam of white petals. Light warm rays of the sun reached her upturned face like kisses, refracted as a fizzy dazzle through the fringing of her eyelashes. She turned to the garden beside her and stared straight into a magnolia tree, the skin of its flowers' stiff curves streaked with a sexual crimson. She was transported by the light and the trees, and just as her child self had once played the miniature warrior heroine down green alleys, so she saw herself now floating in this soft sunshine, moving like a panther into the long jewelled narrative which was her future.

Choice landscapes and triumphs and adventures quivered, quaintly framed there in the zigzag light like pendant crystals on a chandelier. There was the asterisk trail of a shooting star, on and on for years until it petered out at about thirty-three or thirty-four, leaving her at some point of self-apotheosis, high and nobly invulnerable, one of Tiepolo's ceiling princesses looking down in beautiful amusement from a movie-star cloud. This was about as far as any of the novels and films took her too.

A pleasurable sigh escaped her as the vision faded, and she started walking again, on past the tranquil houses, the coloured glass in a hall window staining the domestic light, a child's bicycle propped against the trunk of a standard rose. She sensed babies breathing in cots in upstairs rooms, and solitary women becalmed somewhere downstairs, chopping fruit or on the telephone organising some toddler tea. It really was suburban purdah round here. They were like battery hens, weren't they, rows of identical hutches, so neat and tidy and narrow-minded. Imagine staying in all day, stewing in your own juices. Weren't they bored out of their skulls? It was beyond her comprehension.

And so *materialistic*, she scoffed, observing the pelmetted strawberry-thief curtains framing a front room window; so *bourgeois*. Her cousin had recently travelled India for six weeks on £200, taking nothing but a change of clothes and a pair of sandals. It was brilliant, she'd said, dirt cheap.

> *The world is too much with us; late and soon,*
> *Getting and spending, we lay waste our powers*
> *Little we see in Nature that is ours;*
> *We have given our hearts away, a sordid boon!*

Although after a good patch of freedom she fully intended to pursue a successful career, the way ahead paved by her future degrees in Business Studies and Marketing Skills. But she would never end up anywhere like here. No! It would be a converted warehouse with semi-astral views and no furniture. Except perhaps for the ultimate sofa.

Jade rounded the corner into the next road, and suddenly there on the pavement ahead of her was trouble. A child was lying flat down on its back screaming while a man in a boiler suit crouched over it, his anti-dust mask lifted to his forehead like a frogman. Above them both stood a broad fair woman, urgently advising the child to calm down.

'You'll be better with a child than I am,' said the workman gratefully as Jade approached, and before she could agree – or disagree – he had shot off back to his sand-blasting.

'She's stuck a lentil up her nose,' said the woman crossly, worriedly. 'She's done it before. More than once. I've got to get it out.'

She waved a pair of eyebrow tweezers in the air. Jade glanced down at the chubby blubbering child, her small squat nose and mess of tears and mucus, and moved away uneasily.

'We're always down at Casualty,' said the mother, as rapidly desperate as a talentless stand-up comedian. 'Last week she swallowed a penny. Casualty said, 'A penny's OK, wait for it to come out the other end.' Which it did. But they'd have had to open her up if it had been a five pence piece, something to do with the serration or the size. Then she pushed a drawing-pin up her nose. They were worried it might get into her brain. But she sneezed it out. One time she even pushed a chip up her nostril, really far, and it needed extracting from the sinus tubes.'

Jade gasped fastidiously and stepped back.

'Maybe we should get her indoors,' suggested the woman, her hand on Jade's arm. 'It's that house there across the road.'

'I don't think . . .' started Jade.

'The baby, oh the baby!' yelped the woman. 'He's in the car. I forgot. I'll have to . . .'

Before Jade could escape, the woman was running like an ostrich across the road towards a blue Volvo, its passenger door open on to the pavement, where from inside came the sobbing of the strapped-in baby. Jade tutted, glancing down at her immaculate clothes, but she had no option really but to pick up the wailing child and follow the mother. She did not want to be implicated in the flabby womanyness of the proceedings, and stared crossly at this overweight figure ahead of her, ludicrously top-heavy in its bulky stained sweatshirt and sagging leggings.

Closer up, in the hallway, her hyperaesthetic teenage eyes observed the mother's ragged cuticles, the graceless way her heels stuck out from the backs of her sandals like hunks of Parmesan, and the eyes which had dwindled to dull pinheads. The baby in her arms was as dark red as a crab apple from bellowing, but calmed down when a bottle was plugged into its mouth.

It was worse in the front room. Jade lowered her snuffling burden to the carpet and looked around her with undisguised disdain. The furniture was all boring and ugly while the pictures, well the pictures were like a propaganda campaign for family values – endless groupings on walls and ledges and shelves of wedding pictures and baby photos, a fluttery white suffocation of clichés.

The coffee table held a flashing answerphone and a hideous orange Amaryllis lily on its last legs, red-gold anthers shedding pollen. Jade sat down beside it and traced her initials in this yolk-yellow dust with her finger tip.

'I used to love gardening,' said the woman, seeing this. 'But there's no time now. I've got an Apple up in the spare room, I try to keep a bit of part-time going during their naps. Freelance PR. Typing CVs.'

She waved the tweezers again and knelt above her daughter on the carpet.

I wouldn't let you loose on my CV, thought Jade, recoiling. Not in a million years. It'd come back with jam all over it.

The little girl was quite a solid child and tried to control her crying, allowing herself to be comforted in between the probings inside her face. But she was growing hotter, and when, at the woman's request, Jade unwillingly held her, she was like a small combustion engine, full of distress.

'See, if I hold her down, you have a try,' said the woman, handing her the tweezers.

Jade was appalled and fascinated. She peered up the child's nose and could see a grey-green disc at the top of one fleshy nostril. Tentatively she waved the silver tongs. Sensibly the child began to howl. The mother clamped her head and shoulders down with tired violence.

'I don't think I'd better do this,' said Jade. She was frightened that metal inside the warm young face combined with sudden fierce movement could be a disastrous combination.

The woman tried again and the walls rang with her daughter's screams.

'Oh, God,' she said. 'What can I do?'

'Ring your husband?' suggested Jade.

'He's in Leeds,' said the woman. 'Or is it Manchester? Oh dear.'

'Ha,' said Jade. You'd think it was the fifties, men roaming the world while the women stayed indoors. The personal was the political, hadn't she heard?

'I've got to make a phone call to say I'll be late,' said the woman, distracted yet listless. She seemed unable to think beyond the next few minutes or to formulate a plan of action, as though in a state of terminal exhaustion. Jade felt obscurely resentful. If she ever found herself in this sort of situation, a man, babies et cetera; when the time came; *IF*. Well, he would be responsible for half the childcare and half the housework. At least. She believed in justice, unlike this useless great lump.

'Why don't you ring Casualty?' she suggested. 'See what the queues are like?'

'I did that before,' said the woman dully. 'They said, "Try to get it out yourself."'

'I'm sorry,' said Jade, standing up. 'I'm on my way to an interview. I'll be late if I stay.' People should deal with their own problems, she wanted to say; you shouldn't get yourself into situations you can't handle then slop all over everybody else.

'Yes,' said the woman. 'Thank you anyway.'

'You could ring the doctor,' said Jade on the way to the front door. 'Ask for an emergency appointment.'

'I'll do that next,' said the woman, brightening a little; then added suddenly, 'This year has been the hardest of my life. The two of them.'

'My mother's got four,' said Jade censoriously. '*And* a job. Goodbye.'

She turned with relief back into the shining spring morning and started to sprint, fast and light, as quick off the blocks as Atalanta.

you go, girl! – young women say there's no holding back

Momtaz (17 years old)

My mum is one of the liveliest characters imaginable. She's a whole soap opera in one. Leaving home as a teenager and being shipped abroad with a husband and child is a remarkable achievement. It wasn't all that romantic. Cleaning nappies and making shirts for 25p that sell in high street shops for £35 is not the most ideal lifestyle, but she survived it and now she's settled and happy. My parents share a lot of chores. We've got an allotment, and my dad brings home all the food. He grows everything. And my mum helps him, planting seeds and picking crops and stuff. That's one of the most important things in the house, the allotment. It brings the food. Things like cleaning, my mum's going to do that, but then my dad always cleans the toilet. I don't think he'd let my mum clean the toilet. That's his main duty, while my mum's is cooking. They both mow the lawn, they both paint the house, they share the chores.

In Asian homes when parents are bringing up their kids, they'll always teach the girls how to cook and to do housework, and they never ever teach the boys. And that's how boys grow up, always having a mother figure doing it for them, and when they're older, I think that's why they just presume that the woman's always always done it so why should they do it now. And I think if parents brought up kids equally and gave them both house-work, and if you were an eight-year-old boy and you were told to do the hoovering, then it would register when you're older, it would be something natural. So I think you need to start from a young age.

I respect my parents because they've made so many compro-mises for me, though sometimes it is difficult for me to talk to them and explain my point of view. They don't understand that I need some of my own space, like going out clubbing and stuff. It's like that with most parents but I think Asian parents are particu-larly obsessed with caring too much about their kids. It comes from having such close family bonding.

I'm also planning on having some children. I'm considering eleven – ten girls and one boy. I will bring up my kids differently from the way I was brought up. I want them to have some free-dom. I'm going to let them have their social life. I'll say that now and I'm going to stick to it. I'm going to give them more choices than my parents let me have.

I'm not against arranged marriages. They sound prehistoric and irrelevant to most people but I don't mind if I have one. My only concern is that I know my parents have bad taste in men! But they will let me find my own husband. The only thing they're con-cerned about is religion. They don't care about his colour as such, they just want him to be the same religion. Which I respect, but I think you can have mixed religion marriages. I think it's fine to have kids if you're not married. And I think it's fine to live with a man without being married.

I went to a girls' school, but I opted for a mixed sixth form college because I wanted to get a different outlook on life. When I got to college, I found it easy to make male friends. It's fine, it's just normal. I expect the same of my male friends as I do of my female friends. They have to be there for you. My female friends are great company. I've got a wide range of mates, some of my Asian friends wear traditional clothes while others are obsessed with designer labels and some wear hijab [modest Islamic dress] and cover their hair. I think that being a girl is great because there's so much choice in what you can wear and how you do your hair and stuff. Being an Asian girl is particularly handy because you have the excuse to wear the loudest, brightest and most garish colours. Asian girls are taught to take pride in their appearance from a young age. I got my ears pierced when I was a toddler and was wearing eyeliner when I was five.

Feminism has a reputation for being a power trip for women which I think is negative. But I think if it's going to be something positive it should just be about women being happy with who they are, being proud to be female. That's how I see it. I think it's good that feminism is around because a lot of women need something to help them to become more confident, and feminism is doing that. I don't think Girl Power and feminism are the same thing, because Girl Power is just a marketing ploy and feminism has been going on for years. If you look back to the suffragettes, that was the beginning of the feminist movement.

I think thirty years ago women would have found it a lot more difficult to be who they were because they were listening more to people saying you've got to do this, you've got to do that. Women have become a lot more strong-minded over the last thirty years. They know what they want. They know their goals. And I think they're trying harder to achieve them. I think things will go on changing over the next thirty years. I think women are going to get a lot stronger and achieve a lot more things. There will be women in a lot more jobs. There hasn't even been a female commissioner for the police force yet. I can see women getting roles like that over the next thirty years. And in the home, you see things changing. My next-door neighbour, for example. A couple of years ago his wife was working and he was at home looking after the kid. And I thought that was quite good. He actually brought the child up and taught him everything.

I think it's a positive move for the government to get more single mums to work. I don't think you can force them into going to work, but there's a lot of single mums who probably want to get to work and maybe it's an opportunity for them that they might not have had before. I don't think it will change the family set-up. It should enhance it because it gives them something else, you know, instead of just having the home. If you've got a job it's a whole new aspect to your life and it should be a positive thing.

I don't think that if mothers go out to work it harms the family, though my mother has always been at home. She works twenty-four hours a day looking after us and making sure there's always hot food on the table and things like that.

My ambition is to be a film director. When I leave school, I want to go to university to do a degree, and then various jobs and work my way up until finally I have my own film company. There are female film directors around, but it is predominantly a male profession. Women who make films are often labelled 'feminist film-makers', making films for women. But I don't intend to do that. I just want to make ordinary films.

The opportunities I've had are different to my mum. I've been educated and hope to go to university and get a degree and a good job. But at my age my mum emigrated to a different country, had to adjust, and had a new family. My mum has experienced a journey I never will and I admire her for that.

(Interviewed by Children's Express)

you go, girl! – young women say there's no holding back

Erica Rutherford (16 years old)

I live with one parent, my mother. My dad comes to our house and we go to his so we see each other a lot, plus I see my gran – his mum – every week, so I am close to both sides of my family. But it's not the same as having him at home. When my dad moved out, it was like there was this place that needed to be filled and it's my sister now takes that role, so although she's my sister, she's also like a second parent. My views on marriage are different to my parents because my mum and my dad weren't married. I think it's important to get married. Single parents can do just as good a job but they have a harder time. I don't think it's fair that children have one parent and I don't think it's fair on that one parent either, because they have a very hard time bringing up children on their own, having just one income.

I think women need men to bring up children, and vice versa.

I think your children need to have a balance. I find that if I'm in a new environment and there's girls around I can get to know them, much quicker than I get to know guys. Because my dad moved out when I was at a young age I haven't gained that ability to chat to guys so easily, as it doesn't come naturally to me. When I was young, all I knew was to cuss guys and I was just like horrible to guys. I've changed that now because I realised what I was doing. I think kids need that balance. I think they need to know how to get on with the other sex and it's not going to happen if you're just with women all the time or whatever.

Feminism to me is making sure that you're not put at a disadvantage because of your sex. I think all women can be feminists. So I would call myself a feminist. It doesn't matter where you're coming from or what you're doing. Some people look down on housewives because they say that they are dependent and don't have equal opportunities. But you can't force these things on people and expect them to be happy when it's not what they want. Housewives can be feminists as long as they're happy with what they're doing. Feminism has negative connotations – that it's all lesbians and man-haters – but I'm more with the people who believe that feminism is about women becoming equal to men and having positive roles. Women my age are very aware of feminism. We learn about feminism partly from school, where we hear about the suffragettes and so on. But also from the media, the idea of Girl Power – you can't get away from it. It's not just the Spice Girls, but other Girl Power type bands, American ones like Destiny's Child and En Vogue and British ones like All Saints. I'm not one for role models but I think women like that are important for other women. It's about standing up for your rights and making sure you're not put down.

My mum's always worked. She was working when I was young and I thought it was good. I felt I wanted to do that, to sit down at a desk and have a job. It can be inspiring. My mum's worked very hard – if anyone is my role model it would probably be my mum. I'm an ambitious person, and I feel if I don't succeed in one thing, then I'll try another. She's helped me to realise that it's important to work hard and move forwards.

Women's roles have really changed over the past thirty years. They can be working as a police officer, they don't have to be at home having twelve children. But it's not all progress. I think some things are just being changed for the sake of it, that some women are doing things just because guys can do them. They're following guys doing their silly stuff. At the beginning it was about getting to an equal level. Women would say, 'If men work at a newspaper, why can't I work at a newspaper', and so on. Now it's getting to the point where it's like. 'Oh, if men can walk around with no shirts on when they're boxing, why can't we walk around with no shirts on when we're boxing', and it's just really silly and it's not the point.

As far as things go now; obviously you want to give women a helping hand, but at the same time, there's not much point in reversing what's going on and putting men in the place where women were, where they are not using their potential. It's going to take men a little while to get used to all the changes. I'm not a man obviously, but I'm just thinking how it would be for me, if all of a sudden I was just kicked out of my high chair and set on the floor, you know, someone else took my high chair. I would be a bit upset and confused, thinking, What's going on here? I'd probably get depressed. I could imagine that the widespread depression of men is them just saying, 'I want my high chair back'.

In Parliament I think you do need more women. I like Madam Speaker. I've been to Parliament when I was doing my work experience and she's telling them to shut up and all the rest of it, and she's really funny. If I was a Girl Power type of person, I would say, 'Yeah! Girl Power to it'. She's just taking no rubbish. I think at this point they do need more women in there, to make a balance. I think there does need to be that balance in Parliament, because Parliament is for the whole country, they are meant to be standing up for everyone. So for that reason I think selecting women from all-women shortlists is OK, I don't see why not, if it's going to get an equal amount of women in there.

I did want to be a journalist. I did my work experience at the *Observer*, and I thought, do I want to work in that environment? Like, it was very male-dominated. I don't know if I would feel comfortable in that situation. My life is at this moment very orientated to women, I'm just surrounded by girls all the time and I don't know if I can easily just go into a very male-dominated area. I do get on with guys, don't get me wrong, but just going into a place with that many men around me all at one time, I don't know if I could cope.

I don't think there are jobs that boys are better at than girls and the other way round. I suppose there are things like lifting weights that guys might find easier than girls, but at the same time, I don't think that makes them better at it. Taking care of children is something that girls have a more natural instinct for. But that's not an excuse for men just to leave it up to the women. It's an equal job and it should be a shared job.

The Government is obviously keen to get more single parents into work. I think that people in that position should work if they are able to, but I don't think that it should be expected of them to work 9 to 5 jobs. I think it's very important that children are with their parents a lot. I don't think it should be said that single parents are just taking up welfare and the best thing is to get them working as soon as possible.

I think that both boys and girls should look good. Boys take more care over their appearance now than they used to. I know society places importance on the idea that women should look a certain way and men should look a certain way. But this guy I know works out a lot and he's always asking me, 'Oh, are my arms so strong and are my legs so tough', and all this other stuff. I'm just like, 'I don't care because mine aren't', and then he's like, 'Yeah, but it's different, you're a girl, you don't have to have solid arms and solid legs', and all the rest of it. Society says that women should be one way and men should be another way, that men should work out and women should be thin, but men don't have to be thin and women don't have to work out, so you know, there's different ways that they have to look good. I don't think it's fair to say that's just the media. Because the media, the people who make up the media are only people anyway. It's not like they're aliens or something from a different planet that's forced this on to us humans.

Are girls under more pressure than they used to be? No. I think girls are a bit more confused than they used to be, because before it was like, there was just rules and it was like – like when they had their school dances – you'd just sit down, a guy asks you to dance, you can get up for a dance, if you want to, or you could say no, and that's it. Nowadays, it's like a guy can smile at you, and it's like: Mm, does he like me, or is he just being friendly? and it's like all of a sudden signs have different meanings and people don't know what things are. But I think girls are probably under less pressure, because they're not expected to make cakes and all that, like they used to.

(Interviewed by Children's Express)

still rising

Jenny McLeod

When she was in her mid twenties my mother, like thousands of other West Indian women, left Jamaica and came to Britain. She has now lived here for forty years, as the remarkable centre of our family life: the mother to five girls, grandmother to four girls and two boys, and wife to one man. I don't know when it was that I realised my mother had left her island in the sun to travel thousands of miles to work and live in a country of which she had little practical knowledge, but I always knew the reason why. She came because she wanted a better life and, just as importantly, she wanted a better life for her children.

When my mother came to Britain and found the notice, *No blacks, no Irish, no dogs*, in the windows of the houses she rang the doorbells of looking for a room to rent, she stayed. She stayed because black women have always known that they had to push their lives on, and that if they stood still and accepted what was given them, it would never be enough. From being dragged kicking and screaming in chains across the Atlantic in the filthy pit of a ship to the Caribbean, to catching a BOAC to Britain in the fifties and sixties, black women have known they can't just accept what is given. And with this knowledge they have always worked to move forward.

When I talk to my mother and women of her generation I hear them say that feminism and sexual politics – as defined by white women and a society that they own – has always been the playful preserve of 'skinny white women' who had both the time to sit around and theorise and then the means to put those theories into practice. My mother and her friends found when they came to this country that their feminism was nothing like what the white women believed. Regardless of economic status, their beliefs were intrinsically different. My mother believed in her hopes and desires for her daughters first and foremost – believing rightly or wrongly that within their future freedom and future choices would come her own. In the full sense of what it means to raise a child, she raised all her children alone, with little help from my father. But the focus of her feminism wasn't around the narrow issue of getting men to do the washing up or to change a nappy or two. It wasn't a battle of the sexes in that traditional Western way. Instead the feminism of my mother and the women of her generation was born from a knowledge they carried within themselves, something they learnt about at the feet of their own mothers and their mothers before them: racism and inequality.

When my mother arrived in Britain she had no idea what she was coming to. She arrived in the middle of November dressed for the Jamaican climate she had just left, she arrived believing she was wanted and would be welcomed by the English. She had come looking for freedom and a wealth to take back to Jamaica and in many ways she found a greater hardship in Britain than the hardship she had left behind. It was not long before she realised that a practical freedom had been lost to her the minute she had boarded that plane. She had come from a culture where you hung out, where you worked and played outdoors in the sun; and come into a culture where you went to work in the freezing cold, did what you had to do and then scurried back to huddle around a paraffin lamp in one room of a damp, cold house that you shared with a dozen or more other people.

And this new life put immense pressure on the relationship that West Indian women had with their men.

When I was growing, my mother and her friends frequently got together around the kitchen table and the main topic of discussion was always some man and how wort'less he was, and how he was never gonna change, and how he had no ambition and never would have none. If it wasn't my mother's story, then it was some other woman's story, and the stories were easily interchangeable between those women. Stories like the one about the man who kept two women, got found out and had to choose between them. He planned the wedding, and promised finally to marry one of them and remain faithful and committed to her. The only thing was he planned a wedding with each woman, while reassuring each that he had made his choice and she was it. 'Up to the week,' as my mother and her friends tell the story, 'up to the day, the hour even, that wort'less man with no ambition never know which woman him was going married to and him relative them had to distribute themselves between the two churches, depending on which woman they favoured, hoping that the dirty man would turn up and marry one.' Then there were stories of some other man who weekly put down some woefully inadequate sum of money for his wife to feed and clothe his children and keep the house too, while he went off drinking every evening and weekend, returning home whenever he chose, expecting meals and clean clothes. Or the stories about how another man had beaten his wife 'so till she was as soft as porridge, or like she was nothing but him pickney'.

It is an obvious truth that black men have always struggled with the same quandary as black women: how to go forward in a world that hates them. Black men have chosen to deal with that differently, and hand in hand with that struggle is the struggle they've had with themselves as proud, masculine men. There can be no men on the face of the earth who wear more jewellery than black men do, who paint and ornament themselves to such a degree, who insist on wearing the best suits. The men of my father's generation arrived in Britain proud and dapper and full to the brim with hope at the prospect of work and returning Home in five years with the means to a 'better life'. What they found in fifties and sixties Britain was ingrained state-mobilised racism and they found it pitched against them. It left them feeling useless and hamstrung, without masculinity, without pride, and traumatised by their inability to fight back. First they internalised their fears and frustrations and then they turned them outwards and on to those closest to them: their wives and children. They were sexually promiscuous, they were abusive.

My mother believes the men saw their behaviour as a way of regaining some of the pride and masculinity that had been taken from them upon their arrival and search for work in Britain. My mother realises that the way the men behaved was not exclusive to black men, but the fact that they were in a strange country and should all have been holding together to come through made these betrayals by the men far worse. So the women watched as the men opted out of family life, particularly the support and nurture of their children, and refused the responsibilities life had handed them. My mother does remember that there were men who did manage to hold their own, who did work and who did nurture and provide for both their families and themselves, but they were exceptions rather than the rule.

My mother's two favourite cries whenever she's describing her life are that no man has ever raised a hand to her and that no man has ever come in and asked her where his dinner is. And so into the breach left by the men stepped the women of my mother's generation. They found themselves doing practically everything that needed to be done to drag a family through fifties and sixties Britain. My mother says when she arrived in Britain and found my father, it was she who took charge. She planned how they would go forward. When her children started arriving, it was she who had to find first a room, then a flat, then a house, all the time holding down a full-time job, caring for her children and dealing with life and all that it could throw at her – and she tells me she was not exceptional. These women call it 'To be both the man and the woman,' because that's what they were.

I saw this throughout all the years I was growing, but in no clearer way than when my mother had been married for more than three decades. With three of her five daughters grown and left home, the home where we lived had got too large for the family. After months of explaining the financial sense of a move to a smaller house where they could retire and getting no inclination from my father whether he agreed or not, my mother took it upon herself to move her remaining family and move them alone. 'If you daddy come, him come,' as she put it. She found a new house, sold the old house and arranged a moving day. On the removal day my father still had not given any sign, verbal or otherwise, that he was in agreement or disagreement with the move, never mind going to view the new house. All my mother could do was write down the new address and leave it in the cold empty house for him to find when he came home from work. That evening as we were struggling about in the darkness of the new house to change the fuse wire that had inevitably blown all the lights, the back door opened and there was my father with his suitcase standing in the dark.

That was the story of my parents final move to the house where they now live, but it was a story synonymous with other stories my mother has told me over the years about all aspects of her life with my father. While the women had their eyes on the game, the men were absent without leave. They were having affairs and countless illegitimate children, hand in hand with the children they were having with their wives. The women were planning something of a future around property and instilling self-esteem and confidence in a new generation, while the men were at play – and perhaps because their wives knew there were bigger things at stake they, on the whole, accepted it. In fifties and sixties Britain, black women and black men had fractured relationships as both lovers and as friends. The tradition of marriage and staying put no matter what, living on top of each other in overcrowded low standard housing was not theirs. It was a Eurocentric tradition and some women found themselves marrying and staying with men that a generation later they would've crossed the street to avoid even walking by. My mother believes that the fact that they managed to achieve half of what they achieved and passed on to the next generation is down to the efforts of all the women – and only to some of the men.

My sisters and I, married or single, with or without children, all have a degree of control over our lives that our mother never had. The very choice of whether to live alone or not is a choice that my mother never had the chance to make. She lived with her family in Jamaica, came to Britain and lived with my uncle, met my father and has lived with him and a family ever since. So first generation black British women have begun to take the steps forward and away from their mothers, steps that their mothers made sacrifices for and prayed for. More first generation black British women are studying and studying longer and making real and viable choices in the ways that we live our lives. We have built on our mothers' feminism. The question of what feminism means to us is still grounded in what it meant to our mothers: it continues to exist within our racial struggle, but hand in hand with that too is the fact that our feminism is moving towards the traditional white concept of seeking a true partnership on every level between women and men.

The one area of our lives where we feel very little has changed, and where we would like to see change, is in our relationship with black men as lovers and partners. As I and all my friends were growing up we had it drummed into us that we must find a man with ambition. The first question a mother would throw at her daughter upon meeting her daughter's prospective boyfriend was 'did he have any ambition?' Black women came to this country so that their children could have ambitions and could fulfil their ambitions. They were not prepared to see their daughters with men who had none. But sadly these first generation black British women have found that their men do lack ambition. They have found that their relationships are, in fact, disappointingly remi-niscent of the relationships their mothers had with their fathers. Ask black women what the main problem is with first generation black British men and they will say 'Commitment! Commitment! Commitment!' – or talk about their abject failure to make any attempt to commit.

What our mothers called ambition we call commitment and it is a sad, but widely held belief among us that a man either refuses to commit or he has a commitment and is not living up to it. It is not unusual – indeed some women believe the opposite to be true – for a first generation black British man to live with one woman and to 'keep' at least one other woman at the same time. Sometimes in deception, sometimes in blatant painful honesty and sometimes to keep them with children too.

A very good friend of mine wails to me continually about how she knows that her man of over ten years, with whom she's lived with for eight years, and with whom she has two young children has 'a woman'. My friend knows that 'her man' has two other children with this woman, both of whom are a year either side of her youngest child. The man will neither admit the situation or deny it and she seems powerless to put him out of her home or life. Another friend who has been with her man since school-days, with whom she lives and has a daughter, found out that her man had not only got another woman pregnant, but he had also 'bought another house not five miles from her doorstep and moved in himself and his baby mother', all the while still living with my friend and hoping to continue living with her. Presumably he had it in mind, since the two homes were all but five miles apart, to live between the two, hoping that my friend wouldn't realise that he wasn't around for half the week.

The sad fact about both these stories is that they are neither unusual or any different to the stories of the previous generation. Black men have always had 'baby mothers'. To them it is possibly a statement of freedom, of masculinity. After all, there can be no freedom if you have one woman and you have to return every night to that one woman and lay something substantial down on the table and support and nurture the family. Possibly men with 'baby mothers' even see it as their rage against a society and situation where they can see and find no hope for the future. Simply put, if you consider yourself to be in a deep, deep malaise then resistance is futile and you may as well just go down. If there is a difference between what first generation black British men are doing and what their fathers did, it is that their fathers at least made the commitment of marriage to their mothers – even if that commitment meant nothing in terms of fidelity and duty to the family. First generation black British men refuse the commitment of marriage because today they can. The shift away from having to get married, and having to hang in there no matter what, has created a loop through which black women see black men continually slipping away without facing up to their responsibilities. Black men's perceived fear to commit is becoming legendary among black women. What they see as the black man's failure to commit to one single woman has become the lament and despair of too many black women.

Are women culpable in this depressing situation? Nothing is simple, no explanation for this breach between the black woman and the black man is obvious. And yet a logical explanation is that black women just don't value themselves highly enough to say 'Here so, and no further'. They can draw a line and pass judgement on another woman's situation and say what they would do if they found their man doing whatever, but when it comes to their own life and they actually find their man doing this and that, they don't seem able to step out of the relationship and say 'Here so and no further can you go with me, star!' To draw a line and say what you will and will not put up with within a relationship, and stick to it, is difficult if you don't believe in yourself or value yourself. Why else would either of my friends still be with those men who had lied to them and betrayed them? For all the progress, despite the drive, the motivation, the will for self-determination and the massive journey that black women have made over centuries and even since their mother's generation, it seems that first generation black British women are hamstrung by a basic lack of the arrogant and yet necessary self-belief to shout and mean that cry of, 'Here so, and no further'.

This fracture between the black woman and black man is so wide and commonplace that some women live their lives shrouded in a cloud of fear and loneliness, and the cry of 'can't find a decent black man anywhere!' echoes up and down Britain whenever and wherever black women meet. Of course the relationships mothers and fathers form have an effect on the relationships their children will form. Is it any surprise then that there is this group of first generation black British women who cannot form viable and healthy relationships with first themselves and then men? To trust when you are prepared for the worst is no way to go forward. To put up with something when deep down you feel it and know it to be unhealthy, is equally no way to live. But not to have the confidence to trust when something worth the fight finally comes along is surely the greatest tragedy of all.

Someone very close to me fell in love with a man, was very happy with him when suddenly out of the blue he told her his feelings for her had changed and he wanted out. She was devastated and it took her the best part of a year or more to pick herself up. Now two years later there is another man on the scene who seems like the real deal, but not only does she have her own personal history to contend with, she has the history of her mother and all the friends that she's ever had, all of which makes her afraid of trusting the black man who could be the real deal. Hand in hand with the men that they so frequently dis, black women too have movement to make, they too have changes to make if the pattern is not to be repeated by the next generation.

Some women choose to cut the ties with their 'baby fathers', some have no choice in the decision. Not unlike their mothers these women are doing it on their own, often also holding down a job, and there is now a whole generation of second generation black British children, being brought up by single mothers, who do not even know their fathers. A woman I know has four children by three different men, only one of which has had any consistent relationship with her father – and even that has not been without problems. All four children have behavioural problems. Can that be a coincidence? Their mother either calls on her extended family for emotional and practical support, or has to struggle along alone. She has to cope with four children, a full-time job and running her home. As for the three absent fathers themselves, they are not only missing the formative years of their children's lives but are maturing without a part of themselves that would have been there had they been prepared to stick around and be fathers to their children. If black women and men are to be healthy and happy they do need to stay together and start mending together. Only then can they hope to nurture a healthy, happy, hopeful new generation of children.

Now, rightly or wrongly, some women are beginning to think of their needs first and the ideal second. If they can't meet and find a man who's going to 'come to them correct and with ambition' as they put it, then some are preparing to cut out the middle man and have their children alone. A friend told me about her very successful cousin who has everything she wants materially: the house in a nice part of London, the career that's moving onwards and upwards, 'but unfortunately,' as my friend puts it, 'so are her years!' Her cousin is about to turn thirty-nine, has not found the man she can trust and be with and she wants children. So she has signed on with a particularly exclusive dating agency and has selected a likely candidate – taking into account everything from looks to intelligence to health. She told the guy straight up that she wasn't interested in having anything of a relationship with him; she just wanted someone to father her child. So far she's been sleeping with this guy for two months. A relationship may or may not develop between them, but as far as she's concerned the only thing she wants from him is his sperm.

This all makes sense when you begin to understand that the role models of black women are their mothers, their aunts: the women in their families. These role models seldom celebrate the strong black woman who is out there doing her thing and doing it without children. Their mothers and aunts have been married and they have had their children. When I was growing up, the women who were my mother's friends all had children. Even if there was no hint of a man, much less a wedding ring, they all found a way to have at least one child. Today if a black woman gets to her thirties and forties without a man, without children, it's something to be wondered at by the black community at large and something to be wondered at in a negative and unacceptable way. Their mothers more than likely started having their children in their teens and their twenties, and by their thirties and forties they were finished (my own mother had her last child when she was thirty-five years old). No matter what kind of emotional or financial steps first generation black British women have taken forward and away from where their mothers were, the fear that being manless and childless, particularly childless, can instil in some black women is palpable. It is more than simply contending with biology, it is cultural. Very few women can or want to ignore it.

However, there is cause for celebration and room for hope when it comes to one aspect of the relationship between black women and black men. First generation blacks of both sexes have taken one step forward. They are making friends with each other. Compared to the state of affairs between their parents, and between themselves as lovers and partners, more and more black women and men today are finding a way to become friends in Britain. The majority of the women I know all count men among their friends. These are men that they've known for years, some from school. Some of these are men with whom they've never had anything but a platonic friendship with, a 'brother', and some of them are ex-boyfriends with whom they've found a new way to connect. Once the relationship between them has been honestly laid down as a platonic one, then a mutual respect and spiritual connection takes place between them. Women talk about the different vibe and outlook men bring to the world, and about how they need that in their lives. They feel that their male friends have an altogether more pragmatic outlook on life and they recognise that they and their children need that as a healthy balance.

One of my own sisters, alone with two children, makes sure that her children are good friends with and spend time with two of her closest male friends. All of them seem to gain from the friendship. In friendship then black women find masculinity is not something to be afraid of or feel threatened by. And men, who respect them as friends, have become as necessary and vital a part of these women's lives as their mothers and female friends. On the one hand, women see men as a great source of pain and continual disappointment, while on the other, they see them as a vital and necessary ease within their lives. This seems to suggest that there is a positive way forward and a hope of healing.

Second generation black British women are just beginning their lives. And they are beginning them with even more verve than their mothers. My eighteen-year-old niece has left our home town, moved to London, set herself up in a flat and is studying for a law degree. And she is not exceptional. Talking to her and her friends it's clear that the relationships they have with men are evolving yet again from the generation before. My niece is involved in a relationship that she would call long term, even though her boyfriend still lives in our hometown. She introduced him to our family early on and everyone has respect and affection for him, partly for the respect he shows for her, and partly for the ambition he is showing in his life (he too is studying and has an eye on his future). There is something to be admired even in the way that they are conducting their 'long distance relationship', because even at this early stage in her life she tells me in no uncertain terms that she enjoys a level of trust and emotional support with her boyfriend that her mother's generation and generations before never seemed to enjoy at any level of their lives.

She tells me that she feels that there is a fair number of second generation black men who do respect women as equals, not only because she and her friends demand it of them and seem able to stick to that demand, but also because the men of her age are 'evolving' as she terms it. She says there are young men who do still think they can get away with 'playing women', but the young women of today seem able to stand up to them and tell them that they won't get away it. Probably because, as she says, 'There isn't the desperation between men and women these days as there has been and is for mum's generation.' If that's what she believes of her generation then the future doesn't look too bad. Feminism for second generation black British women means all that it meant to their mothers and grandmothers, but it is also pushing forward even further, beyond anything that existed before, beyond anything that we expected.

sellout

Aminatta Forna

In 1997 a new magazine called *Frank* was launched. Inside the front cover of an early edition the editor, Tina Gaudoin, took an opportunity to assert the magazine's take on feminism with a shot at Naomi Wolf. 'Are we perpetuating the Beauty Myth?' she wrote. 'Only if you believed Naomi Wolf's half-baked thesis that we are powerless to make our own decisions, based on our own personal preferences, about the way we look.'[1] *Frank* is aimed at women in their late twenties and early thirties with their own money and no overt political commitment. Inside the magazine we find interviews with individual successful women: such as the MP, Yvette Cooper or the *Newsnight* anchor, Kirsty Wark. Yet over every page lie the ubiquitous pubescent models, perhaps photographed behind wire mesh, or with a 'blindfold' of the same material, in their expensive kit, their tiny dresses or strutting heels.

Frank is a magazine which has taken a marketing decision, and it probably knows its market, to distance itself overtly from feminism and to promote an image of a strong, sexy woman who laughs and cries, loves, fears, nurtures and ultimately conquers in what used to be a man's world. She no longer needs feminism, that uncomfortable ideology that reminds her of her continuing disadvantage and links the personal choices she makes with her political inequality. *Frank* is not alone. Many women are overtly rejecting feminism, buying (or selling) a line that they are women of their own making, that they can chase individual success and make decisions about their own bodies and their own lives. We currently find ourselves in the middle of a debate over the future of the women's movement in which those stepping up first to plant a knife into the carcass of feminism are women. Indeed, they are those women who have benefited most from the achievements of previous generations of feminists.

Today *Cosmopolitan* magazine, under new editorship, declares feminist theory outdated and about as useful to the modern office girl as Mao's *Little Red Book*. The new editor Mandi Norwood has deliberately re-engineered the magazine in a new independent and individualistic, anti-sisterhood style. Of the campaigning articles of the kind Marcelle d'Argy Smith and her predecessor Linda Kelsey would run alongside the sex items, she commented: 'I didn't feel it was positive or enthusiastic enough. It was pondering on woman as a victim not as an achiever, when women really have a great variety of choices at their disposal.'[2] In the US five young women financiers pose for a series of ads for the underwear manufacturers Jockey. The women are all young and attractive. On the top they are wearing business work clothes; suit jackets and shirts. But below they are clad only in a variety of sheer tights and stockings. All are wearing high black stilettos. The advert declares that these women are not professional models but 'Bankers, Brokers and Traders' from Wall Street. The ads appear

on billboards and magazines such as *Harper's Bazaar*. Women's
rights organisations complain. The models say that it was their
own decision. 'It is about women being powerful, playful and
flirty,' responded Anh-Van Nguyen, a 22-year-old Wall Street
analyst and one of the models.

   In the UK successful women journalists distance themselves
from feminism. 'Does inequality between men and women actually
exist?' asks Anne Applebaum sceptically in the *New Statesman*.[3]
From the pages of the *Telegraph* Anne McElvoy dismisses feminist
activism as 'complaining and proselytizing' and commends women
to 'just get on with our jobs, our families and pleasures'.[4]

   What's notable about this rhetoric of the new anti-feminism is
that it co-opts the language of feminism and mixes it with the glib
catchphrases of popular therapy. Women can make it on their
own merits, won't be told what to think, are their 'own' people,
with their 'own pleasures'. Mandi Norwood declares that she
refuses to see herself as a 'victim' and urges other women, through
the magazine, to do the same. The Wall Street models insist upon
the 'right' to work and to be paid high salaries alongside the new
'right' to dress to an absurdly sexy degree in the office. Women are
still posed semi-naked but now they do so in the name of empow-
erment and not exploitation. When Anthea Turner appeared
naked entwined with a python on the cover of *Tatler*, the photographer described his work as 'a salute to an empowered woman'. A
woman executive interviewed for *The Sunday Times* to talk about
feminism turns the language of women's liberation around effec-
tively and now uses it against the very movement that invented
this way of thinking: 'I want to be judged on my achievements as
an individual, not as a woman,' she says. 'We should not be cate-
gorized by our sex.'[5] The article is headlined 'Feminism? No
thanks, I'm a modern woman.'

   By telling us that embracing feminism is the action of a victim,
the sign of a powerless woman, these new reactionaries would

prevent further changes in the position of women. The public and private rejection of feminism by women who have been the first to harvest the rewards of decades of fighting for equality is different from the attitudes of traditional middle-class women who felt their positions and status, often as the wives of powerful men, threatened by feminism from the outset. But today both groups are taking up a remarkably similar position. Having made their gains the new reactionaries are as keen as the old guard to declare the uselessness of feminism, ultimately at the expense of poorer women who have seen far less radical changes in their own lives.

Today the momentum of change is in danger of stalling because those to whom the torch has been passed have decided to douse it rather than pass it on to the next group of women who still require the support of an active women's movement. The overt rejection of feminism is akin to the denouement in *Animal Farm* when the pigs move into the farmhouse; all women are equal but some are more equal than others. For one group of women feminism has served to allow them to achieve parity with men of their own class and background, and having achieved (enough) equality they declare the battle won. They are declaring victory over sexism.

So the success of middle-class women prompts *Newsweek* to declare: 'It's a Woman's World'. Katrina Garnett, a software company CEO travels to Europe to drum up business and flies her kids over too. Meanwhile the article details job losses to men employed in the heavy industries of the G8 countries including France, Germany and the UK. Soon the world will be run by women like Katrina Garnett. 'As manager of $150 million division of Sybase, a Californian software maker, Garnett was on the fast track. But fifteen-hour days working for someone else just didn't seem to make sense. After delivering her first child in between two product launches and fighting (successfully) for mothers' rooms in which to pump her breastmilk, Garnett cashed in her stock options and started CrossWorlds Software.'[6] *Panorama* asks: 'Is the Future Female?' The tabloids carry tales of listless, antisocial young males one day and tales of go-ahead women like Nicola Horlick the next. We are told that male unemployment is skyrocketing while women are storming the boardroom and occupying the corner offices. The picture is one of female advancement at the expense of male power. In the TV series *This Life* Anna beds her young clerk and ignores him the next day – just like men used to do. This prompts yards of speculation in the newspapers. Is Anna typical of a new kind of female attitude? Male rates of depression and suicide are reported to be on the rise. All this prompts even Fay Weldon to declare in the *Guardian* 'perhaps the pendulum needs nudging back'. She argues: 'Women are financially independent of men: they control their own fertility. In middle-class London, mothers long for baby girls. Girls do better at school, are a smaller proportion of the jobless and are breaking through the old "glass ceiling".'[7]

For better-educated women the great leap forward has been afforded by joining the work-force and enjoying benefits previously reserved for men. 'A minority of women have learned to operate the system as one of the boys,' remarked Yvonne Roberts recently in an article for the *Independent*, 'and good for them while it lasts.'[8] The system is, and has always been, skewed in favour of those in work and away from those who are carers or rely on state support. Between men and women in professions such as law or medicine the gap in pay and promotion is narrowing. So women in those jobs, merely by working alongside men, derive their status and perquisites from the fact that they are now part of an earning, tax paying, property owning fraternity.

The fact that women, having clamoured to be given access to work, now have it, has allowed popular debate on the position of women to ignore work-related issues and, led by the national

mainstream media, concentrate instead on comparatively frivo-
lous lifestyle matters. Self-esteem not socialism is the byword.
Women's issues are reduced to relationships, the laments of single
women, body image, holistic medicine and therapy. Feminism is
thus bled of its radical social or political agenda.

In addition, middle-class women are keen to keep the changes
of the feminist revolution confined to the workplace, and not to
let them upset the organisation of their traditional relationships
and domestic lives. So we hear that more radical feminist goals are
no longer viable because they defy nature. Biological difference
(even determinism) has achieved a new level of popularity
through the medium of media-savvy pundits including Steven
Pinker, author of *How the Mind Works*. It is now assumed that
unequal relationships between men and women are the result of
biology. Many successful women therefore aim to be the boss at
work but a traditional girlfriend in their relationships or a traditional mother at home. We may have laughed over Bridget Jones,
but millions of women bought Helen Fielding's satirical tale
because they identified with the professional, educated woman
who wept over the boyfriends who picked her up and dumped
her. And the same women thrill to the tales of the American television heroine Ally McBeal, another young woman who competes
with men on equal terms at work, but who longs to date them
according to traditional rules after work.

Once women have children, their adherence to traditionalist
ideals is even more obvious. Katie Smith (not her real name) is one
woman I know who buys into the idea of the biological underpinning to traditional ideas of gender difference and domestic roles,
and yet she is a consultant in a London hospital. Her husband runs
a successful IT business. Together they have two children, but
there is no doubt that Katie is the primary parent. It is she who
cuts her work hours, who interviews for nannies, who takes charge
of every detail of running the children's day. She wouldn't have it

any other way. She believes that motherhood is a special calling and that women are better parents than men. She manages her work commitments expertly and tells me, with pride, that the children do not even know she has a job. They think she is a traditional, stay-at-home mum. She does not agree that her choices are limited by external factors, or particularly feel that her husband's comparative freedom is unfair. She is, mostly, happy with her lot.

Other women I know, like Barbara Jones (not her real name), a lawyer with a charity, agrees that this is as it should be. Barbara refuses to take work calls at home, insists upon cooking for the family and reserves the right to call herself Mrs at home, although uses her own name at work. For these women the personal is not political; the personal and the political are absolutely separate. Marketing men, knowing their market, target ads at them. The old Oxo mum has been superseded by the Knorr MP rushing home to prepare her supper beneath the voice-over 'A Woman's Place is in the House'. The middle-class, professional woman can bake her cake and eat it.

Behind each of these individual women is a man whose dedication to the unchanged task of being the main breadwinner has enabled her to exercise her personal freedoms, even the right to push herself to the edge. Between them they have agreed on a form of benign patriarchy in which she agrees to balance the domestic with the professional sphere of her life, at the same time allowing her white, male partner to retain the authority of his birthright. It's when children begin to arrive that traditionalist roles crystallize. Yet whatever the supposed costs of having it all, the economically advantaged, spouse-supported woman has no intention of changing her lifestyle. And many of them recognise this and admit to it. Flora Cohen (not her real name) owns her own company and is married to an architect. His earnings are sufficient to maintain the household alone. She prefers that it be so and has raised their two children herself. 'I would be uncomfort-able if I thought my income actually counted in any significant way. I would not like that sort of pressure,' she observes. She likes the flexibility to do what she thinks is necessary and to do as she pleases. I have spoken to many, many middle-class women like Flora. They like the self-respect work gives them, but do not want to share in the obligations associated with breadwinning.

Reconstructed social Darwinist theories are used to support gendered divisions of labour at home, although (notably) no longer at work. Pinker himself says: 'The sex differences that have been documented are in the psychology of reproduction, not in economic or political worth.'[9] The television series *Men Don't Iron*[10] asserts: 'male brains and neurochemistry make staying at home and looking after children much harder for men.' The pro-gramme features Kevin Beck, a househusband who is struggling with the boredom, the monotony and the frustration of the daily routine of housework and childcare. Sound familiar? Isn't this the identical problem with no name that Betty Friedan wrote about in the *Feminine Mystique*? Women dislike and have complained vociferously and at length about being left in sole charge of all the requirements of running a household too. But Kevin's ultimate rejection of the domestic role is put down to his neurological wiring, his genetic inheritance and testosterone levels. The first half of the programme asserts confidently that: 'It seems as though the human female is built for this job.' Women are better, the argument now goes, ergo women should continue to carry out these chores.

Programmes like these are used to justify the traditional divi-sion of domestic labour that shows few signs of changing. Researchers at the Family Policy Studies Centre, in a study of 6,000 cases (Parenting in the 1900s),[11] found that childcare and domestic responsibilities remained overwhelmingly a female responsibility even in the most apparently egalitarian, dual-earner households. The same study also discovered that, contrary to the growing popular perception of the new, reconstructed middle-class husband and father, that professional men were significantly less likely to be involved in childcare than semi-skilled or unskilled men. Mothers in the study claimed that just 35 per cent of professional men compared to 52 per cent of semi and unskilled men shared childcare. Yet this does not necessarily mean that they are all eager for a revolution in domestic labour. Able to hire nannies and cleaners, the better-off woman is protected from the drudgery of domestic work. This allows her to retain her traditional sphere of power at home and as a mother, whilst also having access to the benefits of employment. The sorts of women whose 'lifestyles' fill the pages of the women's magazines and newspaper feature pages, in as far as they exist, have managed to buy themselves out of the domestic loop by employing other, less well-off women. And having done that, they have no need to try to press forward the feminist revolution.

Where women have trouble balancing the elements of their lives, instead of tackling the difficulties of a new era with considered political solutions, we are offered 'choice'. If 'having it all' was the con of the 1980s, a greedy take on feminism which tried to persuade women aboard with the lure of capitalist prizes at work and the security of traditionalism at home, then the rhetoric of 'choice' is the con of the 1990s. 'Choice' is the easy way out, the way to have feminist principles and avoid looking for real political and economic solutions which all women may share. It's hard to see how a woman today can work the hours most companies now demand and fulfil her conventional obligations at home, so she is given the 'choice' to stay at home if she wants. The idea that she should continue to work, for example, in order to retain the ability to support herself (probably feminism's first principle) is taken as both over-prescriptive and a denial of the natural functions of woman.

Shortly after she launched *Frank* magazine, Tina Gaudoin, the editor who had encouraged us to believe that we were not 'powerless to make our own decisions', very publicly resigned her job in order to stay home and look after her baby. And after Linda Kelsey, the editor of *She* magazine, also resigned her job in order to look after her children, Jeanette Kupferman in the *Daily Mail* noted approvingly of women like her: 'They are the women who took a long look at themselves and all their needs as an individual and managed somehow to adapt to their circumstances. They do not feel at a disadvantage to men because they realise that everything in life has a price: everything is a matter of choice.'[12] In another issue of the *Daily Mail* Diane Appleyard relates the details of her own pursuit of the feminist ideal of having children and yet still trying to fulfil her employer's expectations on a level with any of her male colleagues. In the end she and her husband agreed that she should stay at home. Indeed rather than tackle the work culture she seems to be recommending that other women do the same as she has (as if they all could). The married, financially comfortable woman living in a Western, industrialised culture may not have it all, but she does seem to have more than anyone else. It's a truly extraordinary position in which she seems to be able to enjoy at least three quarters of the best of all worlds.

But to whom else does the luxury of choice belong? Who facilitates these women's choices? Does everybody get the same set of choices? Of course not. The fact is that the ability to choose is underpinned by a male income. He of course, doesn't get to choose. Women without partners, or whose partners are without decent incomes don't get to choose. The state does not provide choice. In fact the state has just set about sending single mothers out to work instead of keeping them at home. Choice has not entered the equation.

Who else can play with the possibility of being a traditional girlfriend or mother at home, and a powerbroker at work, for as long as it suits her? While successful middle-class women are able to feel complacent, to say that they have no more need for feminism, and to feel, as the Wall Street models do, 'powerful and playful', all the evidence indicates that while some women have progressed significantly, a larger number are being left behind. As Helen Wilkinson and Melanie Howard state in their report for Demos' *Tomorrow's Women*:[13] 'Alongside steady advances for many women, there has also been a growing divergence between the haves and the have-nots, the ins and the outs.' The findings of the Demos report were confirmed by Heather Joshi at the Social Statistics Research Unit at City University[14] who reported a widening gap between, on the one hand women in the professional classes who she demonstrated had gained from maternity rights and other benefits and less well-qualified women who couldn't afford childcare, had trouble keeping jobs as a results, faced poverty and had no pensions. Research by Susan Harkness at the London School of Economics shows that while women aged sixteen to twenty-four who had been educated to degree level or higher earn all of 91 per cent of the wages of their male counterparts, women aged over thirty-five with no qualifications earn just 63 per cent of the wages of their male counterparts.[15] And that research only compared full-time workers. Since many women in low-paid jobs work part-time, the true picture of the way less educated women lag behind their educated sisters would be even harsher.

The overwhelming problem with the new image of the women who are outperforming the men is that it compares the status of middle-class women with that of working-class men. Those women who have succeeded in the professions, while highly visible, do not represent anything like the majority. Today one in five women earn more than their partners, compared to one in fifteen in the early 1980s. Great, but that still leaves four out of five women earning less, making it a little early to declare victory over inequality.

Women now make up nearly half the work-force, but most of the work they are engaged in is low-paid, part-time or occasional, scattered hours. It is not choice work and indeed not work of first choice. Here are some of the facts. Of the 9 million women in paid employment, half (4.5 million) work part-time. That is more than five times the number of men with part-time jobs. Of those women 84 per cent say that they do so because of their other responsibilities for domestic chores including, but not limited to, childcare. Michael White, a senior fellow at the Policy Studies Institute who has conducted research into part-time working patterns said to me: 'It is increasingly evident that women are forced into part-time work. They may wait up to a year before giving up and taking a part-time job. Then they get stuck there.' While the numbers of women in management and director positions are increasing, in manual and semi-skilled jobs women are barely off the starting blocks. There is no fear of them reaching the glass ceiling because they haven't even got off the floor. Three-quarters of women work in traditional female jobs like education, nursing, cleaning and food preparation – a pattern which has remained unchanged since the start of the century. Other areas which are currently expanding rapidly and employing more women include retailing, banking services, public services and the service sector (as well as education and health). The fact that there are more women in the work-force has not meant that they are able to choose from a wider variety of jobs – they are constrained first by so-called 'glass walls' rather than a 'glass ceiling'.

And according to a study published by the Policy Studies Institute in conjunction with Joseph Rowntree,[16] few women who have low-status work succeed in moving on into better positions. So it would be wrong to imagine that the success that middle-class women have enjoyed in securing management positions is being mirrored elsewhere. In fact, one could convincingly argue that a large part of the increase in the number of women at work is predominantly due to opportunities in industry to exploit women as cheap labour rather than feminism. Michael White dates the start of the surge of the sectors which employ women to the 1960s, before feminist ideas had really taken grip. What makes this seem even more likely is that we are able to witness similar employment shifts in other countries whether or not they have had a strong feminist movement in the recent past. For example, according to a UN study, in Korea women represent a full 70 per cent of the work-force in health, clerical and customer service work. In Latin America and the Caribbean women now account for between 30 and 40 per cent of the rapidly expanding finance and banking sectors.

With access to good, secure jobs, middle-class women in Britain have been the ones to benefit from such changes as paid maternity leave and career breaks. And the top 5 per cent of working women have seen their earnings rise by a third in the past couple of decades. On the other hand, women at the bottom end of the scale have been gradually losing out. 1.8 million women earn under £62 per week and an average of only £3.85 per hour. They are unlikely to be eligible for the benefits of full-time work including job training, paid overtime, paid maternity leave or pensions. One in three professional mothers compared to one in fifty unskilled working women work full-time.

What about the other claims for women's new, mesmerising power? Do women control their own fertility? The very public eulogizing of women over thirty who are experiencing motherhood for the first time, and stories of women like Diane Blood, pursuing her wish to have a child using her dead husband's sperm, give the impression of complete control. Yet today 13 per cent of women become teenage mothers, and women with poor educational qualifications are far more likely to become pregnant than others. Do girls do better at school than boys? Just as many girls as boys leave school with no educational qualifications at all, doomed to a future of low-status work or years of unemployment. Are women a smaller proportion of the jobless? Yes – officially. But unemployment figures mask different realities. Many women give up work to look after children, but as focus groups conducted by the Fawcett Society showed, would like to work if they could and are prevented from doing so by a dearth of childcare.[17] They do not qualify for benefits (and therefore are not reflected in jobless-ness figures) because their partner may be in work or because they are not, strictly speaking, available for work – one of the require-ments of registration. If they were included they would add a further 2.5 million to the jobless total.

The obsessive focus of media coverage on difficulties and dan-gers (exhaustion, neglected children, neglected husband, no time for oneself) of 'having it all' has completely omitted the voices and the experience of working-class women who, in this capacity at least, are certainly feminism's forerunners. A higher proportion of working-class and immigrant women have held jobs alongside raising a family, have had to cope with periodic male unemploy-ment or an inadequate male wage. Sal, a part-time cloth finisher whom I met in Leeds and whose hours have just been cut for the second time, remarks: 'I read those articles, but I don't recognise my life.' Cynthia says she drives by large houses on her way to work. 'I wonder about the women who live there and I wonder what they do. Is that what their lives are like? I'd like their prob-lems,' she laughs.

Sal and Cynthia's voices are reflected in Demos' *Tomorrow's Women*. 'Frustrated Fran' is one of several archetypal female types used to demonstrate the study's findings. The authors demonstrate the disparity between women of different classes, their experi-ences, their needs and the degree to which their lives have changed (or not changed). 'Twenty-three per cent of women report that they feel angry much of the time – most of them under

25s and in the economic groups D and E, women who have absorbed some feminist values but feel disempowered in a consumer society.'

The logic of the uniquely middle-class ambition to have it all was founded o a premise which took the easiest part of feminism and mixed it with conventional gender roles and consumer power. Education and job opportunities were maximized with a personal philosophy of individualism and personal growth, but this was balanced with responsibilities for children and the home. Work has been discussed not in terms of necessity or economic independence but on the grounds of personal fulfilment, lending weight to a rationale that work for a new generation of women, especially mothers, is an optional exercise which must be justified and measured against her other obligations.

For a woman who does not belong to the broadening middle classes the priorities are very different. She knows she can't have it all – and she is often told she has the right to nothing at all. Her right to economic independence is challenged. In her paper 'Sex Change State' Melanie Phillips condemned New Labour's efforts to shift single mothers from benefit to work: 'The entry of thousands of women into the labour market may well push hundreds of thousands of young men out of that market, thus diminishing the number of men that are marriageable prospects.'[18] And if she doesn't have a partner, the poorer woman is even told she does not have the right to have children. It has been members of her own sex, comfortable in their Victorian conversions with their husbands out at work, who have most recently queued to add their voices to the howls of condemnation. On Panorama's 'Babies on Benefit'[19] (made by an all female team) single mothers were condemned as women who had babies to get more benefit cheques. In the tabloids women writers attacked the single mother as a scrounger and a sponge and stood by when successive governments attacked her. They want to distance their own 'responsible' childbearing from hers. They tell her to wait until she's married to a man with a job (just as they have), even when there is no work for men in her neighbourhood to do. If she is employed she is a neglectful mother and if she isn't she is a feckless one. Economic independence for women was the first pillar of feminism. Genuine reproductive freedom, the second. Yet these two principles are now being reserved for the exclusive use of only those who can afford them.

We cannot foresee whether in a few years time there will be sufficient force in feminism to carry it into the future. But there is some hope. For the first time a larger body of women have access to education and possess the sorts of organisational, advocational and political skills which are required. A third wave of feminism (if the second wave truly is over) will witness other groups of women such as black, Asian and/or immigrant women, disabled women, impoverished women or mothers who still have concerns to be met, successfully recreating the movement in their own image.

There still is a real agenda for feminism. Women are still the main carers of children and elderly people and as welfare budgets continue to be cut are unlikely to be released by future governments from that role. Inflexible work structures have the hardest impact upon the lives of women. Job insecurity plays, and will continue to play, an important part in the work patterns of future generations of women. And that will have a knock-on effect on both financial independence and provisions for old age. The pensions time bomb is a predominantly female concern. Personal safety and freedom from rape and domestic violence remain a source of anxiety for many woman. The rhetoric of New Labour is beginning to pay lip-service to these issues – to the need for childcare, pension reform and support for women facing violence. But the rhetoric is not yet matched by action, and it won't be matched by action unless our culture produces a revitalised feminism.

But the apathy and complacency of the women who feel themselves sufficiently protected from these concerns is in danger of undermining any coherent and cohesive political action. The selling out of the women's movement by women who were once part of it raises the spectre of doubt over the central notion on which a feminism depends – that of sisterhood. Sisterhood is not a natural bond or empathy, it simply requires a sufficient number of shared political concerns. Unless we recreate a new kind of sisterhood, based on pragmatic aims, we are in danger of arriving at the conclusion that middle-class women have the luxury and the capability of deciding that the women's movement has had its day.

feminism and the class ceiling

Livi Michael

May 1995: the tower blocks quiver in the heat. The director has told me to walk towards the concrete playground and stare at the tower block in which I grew up. I get this wrong seventeen times.

A young woman with a pushchair approaches.

What you doing, you? she says.

Is this *Band of Gold*?

Can I be on telly?

The cameraman puts his camera down.

What's your name, love? the director says.

Let's call her Cathy.

This is Josh, she says, toeing the trolley towards us.

Hello Josh, we all say.

Josh's expression doesn't change as he rolls towards us. A small crowd gathers round.

He's my tenth, Cathy says.

You what? says the cameraman.

He's my tenth kid.

You don't have ten kids, says the director.

Cathy thrusts her chin forward and stands, feet apart, like a fighter.

I *have*, she says.

Ten kids?

Ask them, she says of the watching crowd, who nod their heads in unison; yes, she definitely has ten kids.

Come off it.

Cathy takes several steps towards the director. She will certainly hit him. Wisely, he backs down.

Where are they then? he asks.

Cathy is unclear as to were they all are. Two are with different fathers, at least three are in care, one has left home. Josh and another one live with her on the estate.

This still leaves two, but no one wants to press her.

You don't look old enough, says the cameraman.

I'm thirty, Cathy says. Depressingly, she looks less knackered than I do.

Can I be on the telly now? she says.

Later, when I watch the video, it is Cathy who stands out, walking proudly, consciously, towards the camera, pushing Josh, who still wears the same, slightly stunned expression on his face.

November 1996: before giving a talk about writing at a local community centre, I am introduced to the young women present. Beth has fair, fluffy hair, a round pink face and eyes set slightly too far apart. She is twenty-two and heavily pregnant.

My eighth time, she says. But I'm hoping to keep this one.

You have eight children? I say, thinking in a confused kind of way that she must have started at eleven. But this is only her fourth full-term pregnancy; she has had four abortions and three of her children are in care.

February 1994: I am visiting a friend in a bed and breakfast hostel. While waiting for her I am approached by a young girl. She is pretty, with long dark hair. I have never seen her before.

I'm pregnant, she says by way of an opening remark. And my boyfriend doesn't want to know. Do you think I should have an abortion?

Later my friend tells me that Marie was taken into care when very young. Her parents' other children all died in their care, and during her mother's sixth pregnancy a care order was placed on the unborn child in a case that achieved a certain local notoriety.

May 1998: I visit the community centre on the sister estate to the one on which I grew up. It has been set up in an empty shop; next door is a shop that sells groceries, newspapers, sweets, next door to that, a chippy. The windows and glass door are protected by iron mesh and through this a large number of fliers can be seen advertising the credit union, the Parent Action group, a Change that Flat (to a groovy fantastic pad) scheme, Needle Exchange services, a Youth Employment Project and a computer course, run in conjunction with the WEA.

A woman I shall call Linda is on the phone.

Yes, but she's having the baby *today*, she is saying. She's in the hospital *now*. And the eviction order says *immediate* on it.

I have walked into the middle of a Victorian melodrama.

In between calls Linda talks to me.

The centre is open two days a week and two women work there. Government funding to councils has been repeatedly cut, and these days they are funded by the lottery.

Yes, the lottery. Which means that money is provisional and short-term.

Officially the scope of their duties is restricted – housing advice for 16- to 25-year-olds. Unofficially they cover everything, all age groups, all problems, from debt to drug abuse, tackling social services or housing departments, writing references, running community projects (the crèche, the Buzz Club for the under fourteens) or encouraging residents to run them themselves, organising the Prince's Trust and the computer course.

How often do they take work home with them or work more hours than they are paid for?

All the time.

What is the worst problem they deal with?

There is a shifting, transient population. Drugs, debt, crime, propel people into vagrancy. Residents, especially men, come and go. The net result is that children grow up without adequate health care or education; young adults are not registered for the vote or for anything else. They are not on any lists.

We deal with young girls, Linda says, twelve or thirteen years old, who have only really had one year of primary education. They have all the problems – severe lack of confidence, the agoraphobia or paranoia – that stem from being unable to function in the society around them.

All the young girls walking past the window seem to be pregnant. I remember Cathy.

Are there many, I ask, cases of –

(what would you call it – serial pregnancy?)

– young women with many children in care?

If you'd asked me eighteen months ago I'd have said no, Linda says. But it does seem to be on the increase now.

I get back to more basic questions.

Who uses this centre? I ask.

Mainly women.

Who gets involved in the community projects?

Mainly women. On the other estate there are some Asian men who get involved.

So your experience is that even the young women with little or no education, who have babies young and keep having them, want to improve their situation and the environment in which they live?

Linda introduces me to Sue.

Sue has four children to three different fathers. When her youngest child went to school she began working in the school canteen for extra money. Then, when the teacher was desperate for classroom assistance, she volunteered. She discovered that she liked working with young children, that really she wanted to be a teacher.

Didn't you think about being a teacher at school? I ask.

Sue looks at me as though I might be joking.

I never really went to school, she says.

So she started with a basic literacy course and moved on to GCSE English. Now she continues to work in the school canteen and in the classroom while attending the local college two afternoons a week to study GCSE Maths and English (I was just glad I could get on an afternoon course, you know, not night class), and the community centre one afternoon a week for the computer course (you need to know about computers, these days, in schools).

Sue's biggest problem is transport. The college is on the other side of town, about a mile and a half away, and the bus fare is over a pound each way, so she walks.

Distance itself is not the problem (except in very bad weather, in winter, when most of her kids will be off school with one virus or another) nor even the traffic (though she has to tackle a busy bypass, a massive roundabout, a subway), but time. She always has to get back to school in time to collect the kids.

And you want to take a degree? I ask.

Eventually, yes.

What about student loans?

Her face goes blank.

I can't take on any loans, she says.

I refrain from saying that she may have to, from asking her what the alternative is, because Sue clearly needs all the hope she can get.

I'm passionate about this job, Linda says. (Obviously she runs off passion rather than money.) Most of the time it seems hopeless – you're dealing with hopelessness and despair. Then something happens and you realise you can make a difference.

She indicates the new playground, which stands out among all this crumbling, vandalised property like a meringue in a soup kitchen.

The Parent Action group got that, she says. They fought the council – people were trying to block it at every level. Then there was the credit union – that took a lot of work – no help from the council there either. And then, when it was finally up and running, the council asked us if *we'd* underwrite *their* loans to private householders for repairs.

Well.

I walked out of that meeting, she says.

Who can blame her? Some meetings you should only go to carrying a big gun.

I have a few more questions. In the absence of government funding, the council has been desperate to sell off its property. This entire estate is being sold off, not to a housing association, but to a new kind of animal, a private housing company. What effect has this had, I wonder.

The tenants got the chance to vote, says Linda. But the council were desperate to push the vote through. And when you have a shifting population it's hard to organise a vote. Now the maisonettes are being demolished and everyone in them has an eviction order hanging over them.

So what would you like to see happen? I ask, inadequately.

She rolls her eyes. Where to start?

A few years ago, at the same time as the more notorious murder of Jamie Bulger, a young local woman named Suzanne Capper was kept in a house by a group of men and women who tortured and finally set fire to her. Two of the women who tortured her had children, and these children went to a primary school in Moston, where Helen teaches.

Fifty per cent of my kids are Special Needs, she says. We get children at four who can't even talk, never mind do their hour of literacy. It takes us all our time to teach them to say 'toilet' rather than going in their pants.

The school was slammed in the recent Ofsted report. Certain kids were jumping on desks and howling throughout the inspection.

What are the worst problems? I ask.

We have no resources, no support, Helen says. All the special schools have been closed down, but there's no extra help for dealing with these children in the class-room. And if there's a major problem, suspected abuse, the paperwork's horrendous.

One mother kept her little girl in a cage and her other children knew her simply as 'the cage'. The paperwork for that case took months to sort out.

We have a scale of disciplinary measures, Helen says, from reprimand to suspension. But there are some children you can't send home, no matter how destructive they are, because home is where the problem is, where we suspect abuse.

Another major problem is (again) the transient population. Kids in Helen's class come and go, before any impact can be made on either their behaviour or their literacy. Most are from extended families, where the mother has had children with one man, then another, who might bring his own children with him. It is difficult to know how many children are in the family, it is almost impossible to chase attendance.

A third problem is that parental behaviour towards teachers may be abusive.

One mother came flying into school, high as a kite, Helen says. Banging on glass, throwing books around, screaming, Where is she, the fucking bitch? I'm going to fucking kill her.

She wanted to see her son's teacher.

Calming the woman down took over an hour. It turned out that she was angry about her son's swimming trunks. She had forgotten to send them in with him, so the teacher had found him an alternative pair. Something about this alternative pair – colour? size? – had made her very angry. Finally, however, she apologised.

I don't know what came over me, she said.

Temazepan or crack cocaine, one suspects.

Where was the teacher during all this? I ask.

In the cupboard, Helen says.

Who wouldn't be?

Are any of these feminist issues?

Most clearly these are economic problems, the result of the economic policies of the last twenty years. The creation of mass unemployment, cuts in funding to local councils, cuts in benefit for sixteen- to eighteen-year-olds, have resulted in the devastation of communities, the massive sale of council property and the increasing number of homeless people. The kids in shop doorways have had kids of their own by now, heading for the same shifting life. It is important to remember that these things have a history, they are not facts of life. My son, who is nearly nineteen, might be forgiven for thinking that these things have always been, but I hear it from older people as well.

There'll always be these people.

There are some people you can't help.

The poor are always with us.

It is frighteningly easy to forget that fifteen years ago there were not all these people in shop doorways.

Language has not accommodated these changes. We now have a large class of people for whom there is no name. 'Working class' doesn't cover it, 'underclass' is both vague and derogatory. Of course I would notice this as a writer, but the obvious fact remains that without a language it is difficult to communicate. This applies to people who want to talk about this social area, or to people who are in this social area; perhaps most of all it applies to people in it who want to communicate their experience. What do the words 'family' or 'home' mean to Cathy, Beth or Marie? We seem to be divided by a common tongue, to coin a well-known phrase, and it is this, as much as any other factor, that allows the problem to persist.

Divide and rule; another well-known phrase, and one that sums up the overriding achievement of monetarist policies. While class distinctions have become blurred there have never been such differences between classes of people. Most obviously between the rich and poor, but also between the working-class poor and the non-working, between non-working on benefits who are housed and transients, between the working-class in origin who took the educational opportunities briefly offered to them in the sixties, seventies and eighties, emerging with degrees and careers into the *nouveau* middle class, and everyone else.

No writer can speak for all these people. And unlike the heroine of *Educating Rita* I do not think I have a choice about where I place myself in society. I certainly do not think that I have the choice to return to the estate on which I grew up and be accepted as 'one of them'. To 'them', as to most people, I am ineradicably middle class.

My story begins with my mother's, who was a single parent when I was born in 1960. She had left school at fourteen to work, along

with most other local teenagers, in a cigarette factory. But this was
in the war, when opportunities were being created for women,
and when my mother was advised to leave the factory because of
her weak chest, the labour exchange found her a place on a secre-
tarial course. She was good, exceptionally good, at typing and
shorthand, which surprised her, because she had never previously
considered herself to be particularly good at anything. But from
the course she progressed through a career, from typing pool to
personal assistant, until, in 1957, she was working for the government in Germany.

At that time, being pregnant meant losing her job. Back in
England, in Streatham, she lived in digs where 'trains clattered
and banged through the night, the bed was lumpy, and when I
went to cook myself something, the pan was full of crusted baked
beans'. Unable to stand this for long, she came back up North and
took the first job she could find, back in a typing pool.

Still, in 1960, nursery provision was available, jobs easy to find.
I went to nursery as a baby, my mother was employed, it looked as
though we would be settled. But my health was poor, and acting
on the advice of her doctor (fresh sea air), we moved to the coast.
There we lived in a couple of squalid, damp and smoke-filled flats
until my health deteriorated again, and my mother, witless with
worry, moved back.

This time we had no home. I stayed with my mother's cousin
and her four children in their terraced house. My mother slept on
the floor of her aunt's one-bedroom council flat and petitioned the
housing department of the local council daily.

This was 1966, the era of the tower block. The estate we moved
onto won an award for design. The high rise was the great hope
offered to people living in crumbling slums with no toilets or baths.
Though, in fact, in order to get our flat on the seventh floor, my
mother had to prove that she had a job, and an inspector arrived
to check that we had furniture and carpets. Our neighbours were

genteel if anything, an ex-headmaster, a civil servant. It seemed that we could finally settle, that I could stop changing schools.

Then, in the early seventies, housing policies changed. People who couldn't be housed elsewhere, ex-cons, drug addicts, moved into the tower block. For some years we had neighbours who rode motorbikes *inside* their flats, played music so loud that five floors below you could feel your chest bone vibrate through the night, smeared shit in the lifts. We had gang warfare on the stairs, people banging on doors, screaming for help. My mother's mental health deteriorated.

Initially I did well at school, but partly in response to all this I began to slide down the academic scale. I lost interest and began to dream, in a locked-in, autistic kind of way, of leaving. I was going to be a writer and travel (Oh the romance of it!).

Well, I did travel, though mainly it was very unromantic. And I came back and had my first son, Paul, shortly before my twentieth birthday. I lived with Paul, Paul's father, my mother and her cats in her two-bedroom flat for seven months until the council found us another one. It was cold and leaky, and the first week there Paul's pram was nicked, but it was ours.

This was 1980; both jobs and nursery provision seemed to have disappeared. But in a brief period of employment, Paul's father managed to secure a 100 per cent mortgage on a very cheap property. He disappeared soon after, and I was left with the repairs, but for the first time in seventeen years I was out of council housing. Then a friend told me that an access course for mature students had started at a local college.

I had been considered bright at the schools I went to, but that seemed a lifetime away. When I applied to do English and History I felt a lack of confidence so acute that I could barely bring myself to fill in the forms. My first essays were poor. But by the end of the course I had been accepted, not by my local university, Manchester, but by Leeds, a forty-mile train journey away.

I could have moved. But I couldn't have guaranteed getting another mortgage on a student grant, and I didn't want to change Paul's school. So what I mainly remember about university life is being late; trains being late. I remember running into lectures twenty minutes after they had started, leaving ten minutes before the end. But I got my degree, then my Ph.D., and during those years I remarried, and my first novel was published.

Is there a point to this story?

Well, that was my route out. Not for everyone, obviously. But then, it isn't there any more. Grants have gone, cheap property has gone. Like Sue, I would never have taken on student loans. Coming from a background in which there was no economic control, I would never have felt any confidence about paying them back. Other routes have also disappeared. Earlier this century the trade union movement, the co-operative movement, both offered women a measure of economic control and independence. This is not the case now. So where does that leave women in this under-privileged class?

Or, to put it more personally, ten, fifteen years down the line, where would I be?

I do not think I would be essentially different from Cathy, Beth or even (perhaps) Marie. Now that I lead my middle-class life this is very easy to forget. Most of the time I do forget the extent to which I am propped up by any number of social factors – my doctorate, my marital status, my career. My perception of myself has entirely changed, and I am glad.

In my lifetime, in my mother's lifetime, society has opened and closed many doors, like a great heart opening and closing its valves. People are sucked in when they are needed, and expelled powerfully when not.

Again, are any of these issues feminist concerns?

Much has been written about the feminisation of poverty.

Clearly, in this newly-created class there are women for whom all the reforms brought about by feminism, the vote, equal pay, contraception, equal opportunities, might as well not exist (although I have benefited from all of them). It is possible that other changes, the right to abortion, to sexual expression, have had a destructive effect if any.

Do you think women suffer more than men from poverty? I ask Linda.

The answer is an unequivocal yes.

Women feel they have to cope for their children, she says. The Parent Action group on this estate were all women.

But I have noticed something else.

Who comes on to this estate, I ask, apart from residents?

She looks blank for a moment.

Well, just us, she says, and some health workers, social services. Women.

Certainly not the director of housing, who is a man, and who once said to Linda when she rang him up, Who are these people?

Then again, who teaches at Helen's school?

Women.

This makes me think back to my education. When I was at university there were five other mature students in my year, all women. Mature students usually are women, and they are usually (in the North at least) from working-class backgrounds. Teaching is a popular choice of career because they have children, social work is also popular (how many work in the Private Sector? how many in the City?). Now, overwhelmingly, women like these deal with the consequences of poverty. It is as though society knew in advance that it would need people to deal with the problems it was generating, and so created, briefly, that window of opportunity, the grant.

Or am I being paranoid?

But this is not the only reason why women are having to deal with the consequences of poverty. Last week, in a clothing store in Manchester, I watched a homeless man talking to the female staff, becoming offensive. They are polite for a while, but eventually the manager (male) is sent for. He has the man escorted out, then returns to his office.

Two weeks ago, in the building society in my local town, a young man (disabled, tattered clothing) came in and began talking in a friendly but persistent way to the female staff. He seemed lonely, no one wanted to throw him out, women are trained to be kind.

How often does he come here? I asked the cashier.

Every day, she said, with the most resigned sigh.

How long does he stay?

As long as he can.

These are just two examples from my recent experience. I am not a social analyst, I do not have statistics. I'm sure that if a proper study was done, it would reveal any number of hidden ways in which women, trained to be carers, suffer directly or indirectly the consequences of extreme poverty.

It is difficult to see what feminism can do when what is needed is money, jobs, job training, housing, educational opportunities etc. The problem is now very complex, and no one seems very clear as yet about the Government's New Deal, and what it might offer this large and increasing social class (Cathy's ten children, Beth's eight). Feminism asserts that women share certain experiences and are commonly oppressed, yet it suffers, more than most ideologies, from the divisions in this multiply divided society. To women on or below the breadline, whose main problems are shopping for food or watching out for discarded needles in their children's play areas, those feminists who focus on the personal, the mystical, the psychological and, yes, the sexual aspects of feminism might as well be staring up their own fannies without a speculum.

It is true that it would be a great thing if sexual liberation could be translated into something other than the right to have ten children in care, but it is unlikely without extracting women from the culture around them. It seems to me that women reproduce not merely children but the culture in which they have been placed. It is their route to being valued by that culture, however obscure that value seems to be from the outside. It may also be that certain areas of the psyche are too chthonic to be tackled directly; that the urge to do so may have consequences that are as devastating in some areas of society as they are liberating in others.

On the other hand, feminism has a good record of fighting social injustice and women have always involved themselves in social issues, from factory conditions and slavery to wife beating and rape. While eschewing any one form of political organisation, it has been powerful at a grass-roots level. This is the level it needs to work at now. We have too many people theorising about lives they haven't lived, or assuming they can understand complex situations by making rare, anthropological excursions. We do not need individual heroines now, like Emmeline Pankhurst or Marie Stopes. We certainly do not need eugenics, or a return to the sterilisation programmes of the thirties (and later). We need structures and networks which will allow women from all classes of society the possibility of meeting and communicating. Perhaps most of all, feminists need to listen – and this requires a certain amount of humility – to women who may not want or need what feminism has been able to offer them so far.

you go, girl! – young women say there's no holding back

Caroline Abomeli (15 years old)

I live with both my parents. My parents have been together thirty-two years. I'm fifteen. There's five of us. I'm the youngest and the second youngest is ten years older than me. Everybody's a lot older than me, my oldest sister is sixteen years older than me; my parents encourage me to go out and pursue my career and don't let the fact that I'm black, or the fact that I'm a woman, get in my way. If you know any Nigerian or Ghanaian families it's normally, 'I want you to be a doctor, or an accountant,' and that's it, whether you're a boy or a girl. When it comes to careers Nigerian families now see women as equal.

My household is a very typical one, because the man is thought of as the head, but you've always got the woman, running it, in the background. My mother does the majority of the domestic work, although she still works full time. My dad's just retired and so he does more of the sort of building extensions, stuff like that. It's become more equal, I think, because they're in England. I think that if they were still in Nigeria it would be more imbalanced.

My opportunities are much better than my mother's. My mother went to school, but that's it. I think that's because my mother was expected to stay at home and do all the housework and prepare to be a wife more than anything, and I think that's now changed. I mean, my mum's always telling me that I should get my education, go to university, and then I can start thinking about getting married.

As for my grandmother – my granddad had many wives, you wouldn't have that today. I don't really know much about her but I think that just by telling you that she was one of many wives, it just shows that it was a very male-dominated society and she probably had to be there in the kitchen, taking care of the kids, so in contrast, yeah, I've got better opportunities.

Even if I was born in Nigeria today I might not have as many opportunities as I would here, but it would still be a dramatic change. I mean, there's a lot of women out there in Nigeria who are going for what they want, being doctors or lawyers and things like that.

To me, feminism means being independent, not being thought of as inferior to others. Because that's how women have been treated for the past few centuries. Feminism is about a woman being equal to a man. There's no limits. I wouldn't usually call myself a feminist, because if I were to go out into the streets and say, 'I'm a feminist', people would think, Yeah, dyke. That's the bad image that some people associate with being a feminist. But by my own definition, I'm a feminist.

Men are still competing against women and vice versa. The boys in my school, they're so sexist. I don't know whether they're doing it just to wind us up or if they're serious. You get these jokes like: *Why do women have small feet? So they can fit under the cooker!*

What happens if your washing machine breaks down? Slap the bitch!
There is a battle. We have to stick up for our own.

There is a need for feminism now. There's still a lot women
need to achieve. Although we've got a lot of laws in place, they're
not always being enforced. Women still aren't getting the top
jobs. There's still a long way to go until we get what we deserve.

Things have changed over the last thirty years. Before, women
were relying on men for financial reasons and you had to get married to be anything in life. But now women are more independent.
They can say to a man, 'Okay, this is what I want in a relationship,' boom, boom, boom, 'if you don't like it, tough, I'll find
someone else.' And I think now men are starting to get a bit
frightened and thinking, Oh no.

Women have gone from being housewives and saying 'Yes sir,
no sir', and for the highlight of the day to be wondering what your
husband's going to eat for his dinner . . . to having careers, saying
'I want this, I don't want to get married until I'm ready; I don't feel
that society is telling me to get married and that I'll be a bit of a
freak, a bit weird, if I'm not.' And now that we've got birth control, we've got more rights, more of a say in the amount of children
we bring into the world.

Things will go on changing. It might not be as dramatic a
change from now on because most of the biggest steps, such as
being able to vote, have been achieved already. But I think that
slowly the gap will become narrower between men and women.

I think it's important to have more women in Parliament.
Because men have been dominant there for centuries and they
wouldn't know what it's like to be a woman. It's important that we
have women running the country as well. Everybody hated
Margaret Thatcher but I think she had a tough time because when
you have a woman in power she's called a bitch, but if it was a man
it would be like, 'Go for it, you're really doing it.' If it's a woman,
it's like, she's being malicious.

When you have a confident guy, I think that he's really soft underneath. I mean you know the guys that go on as if they're hard nuts, you know, I'm Mr Macho – they're just little mummy boys really. But when you have a confident woman, men often see that as threatening, that cow, that bitch, all that stuff, and that stereotype where men say, 'She's probably a lesbian', if she doesn't give in to his charms then she doesn't like men.

I think it's important that a man should look after himself. I mean, men are starting to go for manicures and facials and stuff and I'm thinking good. Women have always made the effort, doing their make-up and dressing up, and men should make an effort too. They should look smart and attractive and everything. If I were a boy I'd care about how I looked. You see those athletes with their nice, tight bums and pop stars looking tick. They're all doing it!

I want to get married because I think it's secure, not just in the money sense. It's the best environment to bring up children. And as a Catholic woman I think it's pretty important. About pre-marital sex and living together, I personally don't really mind, although the Church does. Though I do think people are trying to grow up too quickly nowadays. I mean three of my friends in my year have dropped out of school because of having babies. The babies are beautiful and everything, but I just think it's such of waste of a life, it's too early to be having kids. Before they've even started doing anything, before they're even sixteen, they're already weighed down with a baby and I think that's such a waste of potential.

I think it's a pity if women think it's equality if they have lots of one-night stands. It's your personal choice but you shouldn't do it just because men do it. You should preferably be in a relationship and maybe set an example for the men. Two wrongs don't make a right. Men are degrading themselves if they have casual sex. You can do a lot better than just going from person to person. The whole idea of casual sex doesn't really appeal to me. However, I think things should be equal and I think women should ask men out.

But I do think it's good that women don't have that pressure any more of having to be a virgin when they get married, of having to wear the white gown. For men, there's nothing in the church wedding to symbolise that a man's a virgin. No one could care less. He just wears a suit, but a woman has to be pure with her white dress, which I think is unacceptable.

I want to be a journalist when I'm older. If I was to go into a woman's magazine I'm sure there'd be no problem, but a couple of months ago I went into the *Guardian* and there were a few women, but all the editors and the environmental editor, the science editor, all of them, they were all older men and I actually felt pretty intimidated by it. I was thinking, Where are the women? But now when you see broadcasts and news on television and magazines, things are changing.

To me, a good life is being able to buy what you want and what you need without having problems. Having a good job and a house and, if you want to, being married and having kids. I think everybody should have the right to do that. I especially feel sorry for single mothers sometimes, because I was watching a programme where a single mother said she would get more money from being on the dole than she would from working, and I think that it is disgusting that you get paid so badly that you can't even support your family. I think they should introduce a minimum wage now, because I think it's just terrible. Like I used to work in a bakery – I know I'm only fifteen and I haven't got a family to feed – but they only paid £2.36 an hour. I've never known one man to work there. And clothes, for example. Clothes have got the biggest mark-ups and most of the people who work in the factories are women and they get paid nothing. There's a lot around my area because I live in Tottenham and if you just go round the back there's a lot of industrial places and they sell clothes and everything, and a lot of the people who work there are refugees and the employers take advantage. It's disgusting.

And I remember watching this documentary about women in Asia and East Africa and they had to be sewn up to show that they were pure – and these were little girls of about three or four. I think it should be totally banned. I mean some people may argue, well that's their culture, that's their religion, but I think it should be stopped.

I think it's a good idea if this government gets more single mothers out to work. Because I think everybody's got the right to work and not just be stuck at home with the kids. I mean, your kids are important, but you need to have a break, you need to have some contact with the outside world. I think it would do any mother good to feel that she's got a purpose, more than just being a mother. And if she got a part-time job, that would be fine for a single mother, she could spend some of the day with her children and the rest of the day her children could be socialising with other children in a daycare centre, and I think that would be good for both parties. I think women should be aiming to do a little bit more than just being mothers or housewives – just to do something more than just revolving their whole lives around their children. There must be more out there. I would not want to be stuck at home with kids, 24, 7, no way.

I'm optimistic about the way things are going now. We're coming to a new century and everyone's optimistic about what that will bring. It will be interesting to read this book back in years to come and compare it to what my children and grandchildren's lives are like. I think I'll look back and see that things have really changed – for the better.

(Interviewed by Children's Express)

notes

the personal is still political

1   *Guardian*, 17 December 1997.
      'In December 1997 the army issued a warning to the troops at
    Catterick army base to avoid sex with two local women, saying that
    they "knew" they were HIV positive and they "strongly suspected"
    the women were sleeping with soldiers.' (The *Daily Telegraph*, 17
    December 1997.)
2   These statistics come from the publishers EMAP.
3   Zoe Ball appeared in the December 97/January 98 issue of *Esquire*.
4   Helen Baxendale appeared in the May 98 issue of *Esquire*.
5   *Fantasy Football* was shown on ITV on 10 June 1998.
6   *Times*, June 1998.
7   The South Bank University, *The Male in the Head: Young People,
    Heterosexuality and Power*, Tufnell Press, 1990.
8   *Observer*, 26 April 1998.

9   *Daily Mail*, June 1998.

10   *Times*, June 1998.

11   *Playboy*, July 1997.

12. These statistics from the Office for National Statistics appeared in *Sunday Times* on 26 October 1997.

13   *Sunday Times*, 26 October 1997.

the thatcher legacy: power feminism and the birth of girl power

1   Thatcher was a pioneer in the truest sense of the word. As our first woman Prime Minister, she made history. For that fact alone, she deserves to be acknowledged and respected, all the more so because it is apparent from her autobiographical writings that she confronted society's (and particularly her own party's) sexist assumptions about women in pursuit of a political career. For more on this see M. E. David, 'Family roles from the dawn to dusk of the New Elizabethan Era' in G. Dench, *Rewriting the sexual contract*, Institute of Community Studies, London, 1997.

2   For more on Conservative feminism *see* the pioneering study by B. Campbell, *Iron Ladies*, Virago, London, 1994.

3   For an excellent analysis of women's voting habits over time, and recent changes *see Winning Women's Votes*, Fawcett Society 1996; *Hard Policies or the Soft Sell: how can the parties best appeal to women?*, Commentary, Demos, London, 1996; H. Wilkinson and S. Diplocks; M. E. David, 'Family roles from the dawn to dusk of the New Elizabethan Era' in G. Dench, *Rewriting the sexual contract*, Institute of Community Studies, London, 1997.

4   C. Quest and D. Conway, *Free Market Feminism*, Institute of Economic Affairs, London, 1997.

5   For more on 'masculinisation' and value shifts among young women *see* H. Wilkinson, *No turning back: generations and genderquake*, Demos, London, 1994; H. Wilkinson and G. Mulgan, *Freedom's Children*, Demos, London 1995; H. Wilkinson and M. Howard, *Tomorrow's Women*, Demos, London, 1997.

6   *See* C. Quest and D. Conway, *Free Market Feminism*, Institute of
    Economic Affairs, London, 1997; J. Bethell, S. Brocklebank-Fowler,
    A. Honnor and A. Reid, *Blue Skies Ahead; capturing the missing gen-
    eration*, Centre for Policy Studies, London, 1997.

7   A. Clark, *Diaries*, Weidenfeld and Nicholson, London, 1993.

8   S. Faludi, *The Undeclared War Against Women*, Chatto & Windus,
    1992, London; M. French, *War Against Women*, Hamish Hamilton,
    London, 1993.

9   N. Wolf, *Fire with Fire, The New Female Power and How it Will
    Change the Twenty-First Century*, Chatto & Windus, London, 1993.

10 For evidence on value shifts between men and women and the new
    female optimism see H. Wilkinson, *No turning back: generations and
    genderquake*, Demos, London, 1994; H. Wilkinson and G. Mulgan,
    Freedom's Children, Demos, London, 1995; H. Wilkinson and M.
    Howard, *Tomorrow's Women*, Demos, London, 1997.

    For an exploration of the implications of the shift to androgyny
    see Tomorrow's Women, op. cit.

11 For more examples of these and other trends *see* M. Howard,
    Tomorrow's Women, Demos, London, 1997.

12 Ibid.

13 *See* H. Wilkinson, *Equality and diversity in a time of change: a case-
    study of regional broadcasting*, Demos, London, 1995; H. Wilkinson,
    *Equality and diversity in a time of change: a casestudy of young profes-
    sionals*, Demos, London, 1995; H. Wilkinson, *Through the eyes of
    shop floor workers: equal opportunities in manufacturing*, Demos,
    London, 1995; H. Wilkinson, V. Cooke and D. Mattinson,
    *Continuity and change amongst 18–34-year-olds: a qualitative research
    study*, Demos, London, 1995.

14 *See* N. Wolf, *Fire with Fire, The New Female Power and How it Will
    Change the Twenty-First Century*, Chatto & Windus, London, 1993;
    R. Denfeld, *The New Victorians*, Simon & Schuster, London, 1995;
    H. Wilkinson, *No turning back: generations and genderquake*, Demos,
    London, 1994; H. Wilkinson and G. Siann, *Gender, feminism and
    the future*, Demos, London, 1995; H. Wilkinson, *Germain's desperate
    bid for attention*, Demos, London, 1995.

15 Women born in the 1960s and beyond are the first to come of age since the great battles of the feminist movement in the 1970s and they have entered a labour market in which a framework of equal opportunities legislation is in place. As the generation coming after these historic struggles, they both take things for granted in ways that are simply inconceivable to older women and also feel less need to fight battles in a strident way. For more on this argument *see* H. Wilkinson, *No turning back: generations and genderquake*, Demos, London, 1994; H. Wilkinson and G. Mulgan, *Life After Politics*, HarperCollins, London, 1997.

16 H. Wilkinson and M. Howard, *Tomorrow's Women*, Demos, London, 1997.

17 B. Friedan, *Feminine Mystique*, Penguin, London, 1993.

18 The ideas underpinning the modernisation of the Labour Party, which gave birth to New Labour, owe much to an acceptance of the virtues of the market, and of globalisation and many of the central tenets of the Thatcher project. *See* for example, The New Unionism, Trade Union Congress Report, London, 1997.

19 H. Wilkinson, *No turning back: generations and genderquake*, Demos, London, 1994.

20 H. Wilkinson and M. Howard, *Tomorrow's Women*, pp. 18–19, Demos, London, 1997.

21 Ibid.

22 Ibid.

23 Ibid.

24 Ibid.

25 H. Wilkinson and G. Mulgan, *Freedom's Children*, Demos, London, 1995.

26 H. Wilkinson, 'Business Feminism', *Demos Quarterly*, 8, Demos, London, 1996.

27 H. Wilkinson and G. Mulgan, *Freedom's Children*, Demos, London, 1995.

28 This is frequently written about in the UK context but was also the basis of R. Denfeld's critique in *The New Victorians*, Simon & Schuster, London, 1995.

29 For key trends *see* H. Wilkinson, *Time out: the costs and benefits of paid parental leave in the UK*; Demos, London, 1997; H. Wilkinson and M. Howard, *Tomorrow's Women*, Demos, London, 1997.

30 H. Wilkinson and M. Howard, *Tomorrow's Women*, Demos, London, 1997.

31 The average age at which women in the UK marry was 23 in 1976 compared to 26 in 1993. *PreFamily Lifestyles*, p. 13, Mintel, London, 1996.

32 The average age at first birth rose from 25 in 1976 to 29 in 1995. *PreFamily Lifestyles*, p. 13, Mintel, London, 1996.

33 The average number of children born per women has fallen from 3 in 1961 to 1.8 in 1995. *PreFamily Lifestyles*, p. 13, Mintel, London, 1996.

34 *PreFamily Lifestyles*, p. 13, Mintel, London, 1996.

35 H. Wilkinson, *The proposal: giving marriage back to the people*, Demos, London, 1997.

36 *See* J. Bethell, S. Brocklebank-Fowler, A. Honnor and A. Reid, *Blue Skies Ahead; capturing the missing generation*, Centre for Policy Studies, London, 1997.

37 H. Wilkinson and G. Mulgan, *Freedom's Children*, Demos, London, 1995.

38 *See*, for example, H. Joshi and P. Paci, *Wage differentials between men and women*, Department of Employment, p. 34. This research on the pay gap between men and women finds that since 1978 the impact of the education and training deficit on women's wages had decreased from 9 per cent to just 0.4 per cent by 1991.

39 The statistics on this are cited in H. Wilkinson and G. Mulgan, *Freedom's Children*, Demos, London, 1995.

40 G. Sheehy, *New Passages: Mapping your life across time*, HarperCollins, London, 1997.

41 The philosophy of power feminism now spans the political spectrum and can be found within a range of feminist traditions – from free market feminism to liberal feminism, to feminism informed by structuralist perspectives (whether it be socialist or radical feminism).

why we still need feminism

1   *Independent*, 4 February 1997. *See also* 'Discrimination against me in the UK', the UKMM, 1995.
2   *New York Times*, 14 July 1996.
3   N. Wolf, *The Beauty Myth*, Chatto and Windus, 1990.
4   Equal Opportunities Commission and Women's National Commission, *In Pursuit of Equality; a National Agenda for Action*, MANCHESTER, 1992.
5   Ibid.
6   Nuala O'Faolain, 'The issues around which feminism revolves', *Irish Times*, 10 February 1997.
7   Women's National Commission, *Growing up Female in the UK*, London, 1997.
8   Earthscan Publications, *The Reality of Aid*, London, 1997.
9   Anne Phillips, 'What has socialism to do with sexual equality?' in *Equality*, IPPR, 1997.
10   For a detailed argument of this case *see* Caroline Glendinning and Jane Millar, *Women & Poverty in Britain in the 1990s*, Harvester Wheatsheaf, 1992.
11   For a detailed analysis *see The gender impact of CCT*, Equal Opportunities Commission, MANCHESTER, 1995.
12   Women have in some cases successfully challenged CCT, for example, in Cleveland, 2,000 female school-workers won a case backed by their unions the GMB and UNISON. The women had individually lost between £5 and £50 per week depending on the hours they worked. Male workers in similar jobs at the same council did not have their wages cut. The women won over £1 million. The original decision which acted as a precedent was *Ratcliffe and others v North Yorkshire County Council (1995)* where three catering assistants from a predominantly female work-force won their claim of sex discrimination when they had their terms and conditions of employment reduced due to CCT. The TGWU has initiated a judicial review against the Government claiming that CCT rules indirectly discriminate against women and were unlawful under

European equal pay law. The review is currently suspended pending the consultation process over Best Value.

13   World Development Movement Report, quoted in *Tribune*, 10 October 1997.

14   Charlotte Raven, 'Women: Me, Myself, I', *Guardian*, 9 September 1996.

15   *See* Imelda Whelehan, *Modern Feminist Thought*, Edinburgh University Press, 1995.

16   *See* Linda Nicholson (ed.), *The Second Wave: A Reader in Feminist Theory*, Routledge, 1997.

17   With the caveat that most working women would not describe their job as a 'career' because it is likely to be low-paid, menial and insecure.

never give up

1   Sir Bernard Ingham wrote about the phone-in in his column for the *Sunday Express* on 8 February 1988.

lesbians on horseback

1   Nick Foulkes, 'Girl Guides', *ES* magazine, 12 December 1997. Pin-ups of 'The New Lesbians' included Hattie Jacques, Delia Smith, Judith Anderson as Mrs Danvers, Keith Flint from Prodigy and Liam Gallagher from Oasis.

2   This idea is further explored in *Lesbians are so chic*: 'Lesbianism is constructed as fiction, fictionalised into action in order to keep the fundamental myth of society – heterosexuality – in place. The disappearing lesbian produced by popular culture is an organised reformulation of the same thoughts so many lesbians have heard, and continue to hear, expressed by our heterosexualised mothers, who echo Freud and the assumed rights of men when they say "it's just a phase".' (Laura Cottingham, *Lesbians are so chic*, p. 4, Cassell, London, 1996.)

3   Sarah Schulman, *Sophie Horowitz Story*, Naiad, USA, 1984.

4   Fran Lebowitz explains in her essay 'Beauty Is Filthy Rich' why
women are not allowed to be ugly. 'In this society it is a hindrance
for men to be beautiful. Well, it's useful for gay men, yes; but gay
men don't have the power. The power in this world is held by heterosexual white men, and always will be. Therefore the value of
every single thing in the world is the value heterosexual men place
on it. These men don't value beauty in men – they deride it, in
fact – but they certainly value it in women. Since we live in a capitalist society, a woman's beauty has value on the open market,
which is why the beautiful women get the rich guys.' (Fran
Lebowitz, 'Beauty Is Filthy Rich', in Dorothy Shefer's *What is
Beauty?*, p. 49, Thames and Hudson, London, 1997.)

5   This rule of thumb was disproved in *Vanity Fair*, March 1998. The
American designer at Gucci, Tom Ford said, 'If I weren't in a relationship with Richards now there are women I'm attracted to. I'd
hate to think they wouldn't consider me as a boyfriend because I
was gay.'

   Shock, horror. Is fashion's top trend meister about to make bi-
curiosity fashionable?

6   *Thud*, pp. 24–5, 22 January 1998.

7   *Boyz* magazine is the cream of the down and dirty gay men's free
press. Witty and clever, it gives the impression that gay men have
found their paradise here on earth. Aside from fashion, style and
some probing problem pages, it has one of the most eclectic contact
sections in the business.

8   Susie Bright, *Susie Sexpert's Lesbian Sex World*, Cleis Press, San
Francisco, 1990. Bright's book caused a sensation when it came out
in 1990, claiming that it would smash the myth of lesbians' 'inher-
ent sexual gentility and monogamous nature'.

9   Valerie Solanas, *Scum Manifesto*, AK Press, USA, 1996.

10   I owe my wash-and-go synopsis of lesbianism throughout the ages to
Lillian Faderman's *Odd Girls and Twilight Lovers* published by
Penguin, London, 1992.

11   Radclyffe Hall often relates her condition to that of a chased fox in
The Well of Loneliness, Virago, London, 1982.

12   The Candy Bar opened in the autumn of 1997. It publicised itself as 'the UK's first girls' bar'. It is owned by a gay man who has handed the management reins over to lesbian friends to manage. At the time of going to press the Candy Bar still forms the hub of the lesbian scene in London. Although gay men are admitted as guests, the management insists that the bar will not go the same way as many other lesbian/gay mixed bars in Soho, i.e. straight people want in on the act and suddenly the bars become 'trendy' and are no longer lesbian/gay.

13   In October 1997, the Government changed its immigration policy to allow the foreign lesbian and gay partners of UK residents to apply to live in Britain. Couples must show that they have a relationship 'akin' to marriage and one partner must be living and settled in the UK. The couple must be able to prove that they have been living together in a stable relationship for four or more years. The Government has not successfully answered how couples are supposed to live together when most countries' immigration policies keep them apart.

14   *Vanity Fair*, March 1998, p. 100.

lentils and lilies

The extracts in 'Lentils and Lilies' come from the following poems: p. 105, lines 45–6 from 'Dejection: an Ode' by Samuel Taylor Coleridge [p. 84]; pp. 105–6, lines 67–70 and 130–32 from 'Intimations of Immortality' by William Wordsworth. [p. 85]; p. 106, book 1 line 301 from *The Prelude* by William Wordsworth. [p. 87]; p. 106, lines 1–4 from the sonnet 'The world is too much with us' by William Wordsworth. [p. 88]

sellout

1   Tina Gaudoin, *Frank*, July 1998.

2   This extract in *Cosmopolitan* is taken from an interview with Laura Tennant in *Independent on Sunday*, November 1997.

3   Anne Applebaum, *New Statesman*, 16 January 1998.

4   Anne McElvoy, *Telegraph*, 22 January 1998.

5   This woman executive was interviewed for the article 'Feminism? No thanks, I'm a modern woman', *Sunday Times*, 25 January 1998.

6   Katrina Garnett appeared in an article in *Newsweek*, 18 May 1998.

7   Fay Weldon, *Guardian*, 9 May 1998.

8   Yvonne Roberts, *Independent*, 8 July 1998.

9   Steven Pinker, *How the Mind Works*, Penguin, London, 1998.

10   *Men Don't Iron* TV series, Channel 4, June 1998.

11   Elsa Ferri and Kate Smith, *Parenting in the 1990s*, Family Policy Studies Centre, London, November 1996.

12   Jeanette Kupferman, 'Having it all', *Daily Mail*, 2 December 1995.

13   H. Wilkinson and M. Howard, *Tomorrow's Women*, Demos, London, 1997.

14   S. Dex and H. Joshi, 'A Widening Gulf Among Britain's Mothers', *Oxford Review of Economic Policy*, vol. 12, no. 1, 1996, pp. 65–75.

15   Susan Harkness: *How would British women be affected by a minimum wage?* Unpublished paper, LSE, June 1995.

16   Michael White and John Forth, *Pathways through Unemployment: the effects of a flexible labour market*, Rowntree Foundation, 1998.

17   Mary Anne Stephenson, *The Glass Trapdoor Women, politics and the media during the 1997 General Election*, Fawcett Society, London, 1998.

18   Melanie Phillips, *Sex Change State*, Social Market Foundation, London, 1997.

19   *Panorama*'s 'Babies on Benefit', BBC 1, September 1993.

notes on the contributors

Julie Bindel
Julie Bindel is currently the Assistant Director of the Research Centre on Violence, Abuse and Gender Relations at Leeds Metropolitan University. She has been involved in campaigning against violence against women since 1979. She is a founder of Justice for Women. Julie has published papers in books and journals, contributes to governmental and inter-agency policy and practice, is a contributing editor to two women's magazines, regularly appears on TV and radio, writes for the *Guardian* Women's Page and runs media training courses.

Children's Express
Karen Loughrey, Julia Press, Erica Rutherford, Caroline Abomeli and Momtaz are all editors at the London bureau of news agency

Children's Express. The girls were interviewed by their peers Koiya Donovan (12), Juanita Rosenior (13), Stuart Fletcher (16), Kathleen Dawes (15) and Rachel Bulford. Children's Express, a charity, is a child-led programme of learning through journalism for young people aged 8 to 18. It regularly produces news and comment for national and local newspapers, specialist magazines and Radio 4 and 5.

Aminatta Forna

Aminatta Forna is a writer and broadcaster. She has reported and presented on numerous current affairs programmes, including the *Late Show, Correspondent, On the Record* and *Public Eye* and the *E-Files*. Her writing includes *Mother of All Myths, Pornography: Women, Violence and Civil Liberties, Conversations with Maya Angelou* and *Black British Cultures*. In 1996 she won a Harkness Fellowship to the University of California. She is a regular contributor to the *Independent on Sunday*, and is currently working on a book about her family and childhood in post-colonial Africa.

Oona King

Member of Parliament for Bethnal Green and Bow, Oona King first entered politics as political assistant to the Labour Party Leader, Glyn Ford MEP, in the European Parliament. In 1992, she was seconded as a researcher/campaign assistant to the late John Smith MP and she spent two years as Glenys Kinnock's political assistant. In 1995 she became a recruitment and organisation officer for the GMB, Britain's general trade union. She was a Regional Officer and Convening Officer for the NHS when she was selected as the Labour candidate for Bethnal Green in 1997.

Katharine Viner

Katharine Viner is the editor of the *Guardian Weekend* magazine. She has also written for *The Sunday Times* and *Cosmopolitan*.

Jenny McLeod

Jenny McLeod is a Jamaican-born writer living in London. She has written several plays and has recently been the Tricycle Theatre's Writer-in-Residence. Her first novel, *Stuck up a Tree*, was published by Virago Press in 1998.

Livi Michael

Livi Michael is the author of three award-winning novels, *Under a Thin Moon*, *Their Angel Reach* and *All the Dark Air*, which was published by Secker and Warburg. She lectures in English and Creative Writing, and is currently working on a fourth novel. She lives in Lancashire.

Helen Simpson

Helen Simpson is an author and the recipient of *The Sunday Times* Young Writer of the Year 1991 and the Somerset Maugham Award 1991 and was listed as one of Granta's twenty Best of Young British Novelists in 1993. She has also been a Writer-in-Residence at the Royal National Theatre Studio.

Stephanie Theobald

After finishing a degree in modern languages at Cambridge University, Stephanie Theobald worked as a journalist in Paris for five years before returning to London where she became fashion editor of *The European*. She is currently working on a novel about living an unseemly life in Paris.

Helen Wilkinson

Helen Wilkinson is Project Director at Demos, a Research Associate at the Families and Work Institute and a Commonwealth Fund Harkness Fellow. She is the author of *No Turning Back: Generations and Genderquake*, *Freedom's Children* (with Geoff Mulgan), *The Proposal: Giving marriage back to the* people, *Time Out: The costs and benefits of paid parental leave in the UK* and *Tomorrow's Women* (with Melanie Howard). Her book, *The Age of Androgyny*, will be published by HarperCollins in 2000.